Experiencing the HOLY SPIRIT

TRUTHS THAT CAN TRANSFORM YOUR LIFE

Jim McNair

Bethany Fellowship INC.
MINNEAPOLIS, MINNESOTA 55438

Bible quotations are from the Revised
Standard Version unless otherwise indicated.

Published by Bethany Fellowship, Inc.
6820 Auto Club Road, Minneapolis, Minnesota 55438

Printed in the United States of America

Library of Congress Cataloging in Publication Data:
McNair, Jim, 1934-
    Experiencing the Holy Spirit.

    Bibliography: p.
    Includes index.
    1. Gifts, Spiritual.   2. Holy Spirit.   I. Title.
BT767.3.M33   231'.3   77-9262
ISBN 0-87123-135-2

To Him who so loved
that He
gave
the Lord Jesus Christ
and His Holy Spirit
for our salvation
and blessing,
and also gave
a wonderful wife and family—
Joy, Karen, Lynn and Peter

James Warwick McNair is a resident of New Zealand. He was ordained as a Baptist minister following two years of Bible college work and four years of theological seminary. He holds an L.Th. degree from the Melbourne College of Divinity.

Rev. McNair has served Baptist churches in two locations in New Zealand, and is currently involved in teaching, preaching, and counseling on an interdenominational level.

Preface

It is sometimes said that the ministry of the Holy Spirit is better felt than telt! There is glorious truth in that and we know what is meant; but it is not the whole truth, for it also tells well. The Old Testament, the Gospels, Acts and the Epistles unitedly testify to this reality and present us with a logical pattern that is basically simple to grasp yet life-changing in its power.

Unlike its companion volume *Love and Gifts*, this book does not consider the text of scripture verse by verse. Instead, it is concerned with vital theological, topical and practical issues that arise out of those scriptures. In the companion book it was generally adequate to make all necessary points within the confines of the biblical passage being considered; but other subjects were so large or involved so many other scripture passages that they needed to be dealt with as separate topics. Hence this further volume.

Some people are afraid of Christian experience. They like to stand back and examine doctrine from a distance without becoming personally involved in it, and they are suspicious and critical of anything that has a subjective element. If you feel like that, you will be disturbed by this book, for while it seeks to be objective in its approach the objective truth in Scripture demands our response, and we soon find that the theological issues are not an end in themselves but are drawing us towards deeper involvement with the attractive and living Jesus Christ and God our Father!

What incredible grace He shows us! Rich though the Lord Jesus was He became poor to make us rich. He came to bless and lavish upon us the riches of His grace (2 Cor. 8:9; Eph. 1:3, 7-8). To this end He sent the Spirit to bear witness to Him, to make His work real in our hearts, and to empower us to follow, worship and serve Him. Small wonder therefore if we have difficulty grasping or describing how God can bless His undeserving children in this way! But He does!

I am convinced that whatever have been our experiences of the Lord, He wants to give us more! The power of God assumes many forms and like the waters of the Niagara there is always more to follow! In these pages I want to share simply some truths which by God's grace and power have transformed my own and others' lives and ministries.

My great desire is that my readers meet the Lord Jesus Christ afresh, be filled with the Holy Spirit and be further equipped to serve the Lord and express their faith from the Scriptures. It is therefore my prayer that this book, together with *Love and Gifts*, will stimulate new interest in the Holy Spirit and Jesus the Baptizer, and provide practical teaching for those who have been baptized in the Holy Spirit for years, as well as guiding those who want to enter into the realm of the Spirit-filled life. May it be food for mind and heart.

God encourages us to cry to Him for a new experience of himself and His riches. Like the Psalmist we can say:

> In my distress I called upon the Lord;
> to my God I cried for help.
> From his temple he heard my voice,
> and my cry to him reached his ears . . .
> He reached from on high, he took me,
> he drew me out of many waters.
> He delivered me from my strong enemy . . .
> *He brought me forth into a broad place*
>
> (Ps. 18:6, 16-17, 19).

Contents

Acknowledgements

We gratefully acknowledge our indebtedness to the following publishers and/or authors for permission to use quotations from their works:

Acts of the Apostles by F. F. Bruce, © 1953, published by Wm. B. Eerdmans Publishing Co., Grand Rapids, Mich.

Ante-Nicene Fathers, © 1956, published by Wm. B. Eerdmans Publishing Co., Grand Rapids, Mich.

A New Testament Commentary, edited by G. C. D. Howley, F. F. Bruce, H. L. Ellison, © 1969, published by Zondervan Publishing House, Grand Rapids, Mich.

A Theology of the Holy Spirit by F. D. Bruner, © 1970, published by Wm. B. Eerdmans Publishing Co., Grand Rapids, Mich.

Baptism in the Holy Spirit by James D. G. Dunn, © 1970, published by Alec. R. Allenson, Inc., Napperville, Ill.

Baptism and Fullness by John R. W. Stott, © 1975, published by Inter-Varsity Press, London, and Downers Grove, Ill.

Book of the Acts by F. F. Bruce, © 1954, published by Wm. B. Eerdmans Publishing Co., Grand Rapids, Mich.

Epistle of Paul to the Romans by C. H. Dodd, © 1932, published in the *Moffatt N.T. Commentary* by Hodder & Stoughton, London, and Harper & Row, New York, N.Y.

Epistles to the Ephesians and the Colossians by E. K. Simpson and F. F. Bruce, © 1957, published by Wm. B. Eerdmans Publishing Co., Grand Rapids, Mich.

Epistle to the Romans by C. K. Barrett, © 1958, published by Harper & Row, New York, N.Y.

First Epistle to the Corinthians by C. K. Barrett, © 1968, published by Harper & Row, New York, N.Y.

Jesus and the Gospel by James Denny, © 1908, New York, N.Y.

Reflected Glory by Thomas A. Smail, © 1975, by Thomas A. Smail, published by Wm. B. Eerdmans Publishing Co., Grand Rapids, Mich.

Spiritual Gifts and the Church by D. Bridge and D. Phypers, © 1973, published by Inter-Varsity Press, London, and Downers Grove, Ill.

The Baptism in the Holy Spirit by Harold Horton, undated, published by Assemblies of God Publishing House, Nottingham, England.

That Incredible Christian by A. W. Tozer, © 1964, published by Christian Publications, Inc., Harrisburg, Penna. 17101.

Towards a New Testament Understanding of Baptism in the Spirit by L. D. Guy, Auckland, New Zealand, unpublished paper.

Word Studies in the New Testament by M. R. Vincent, © 1972 edition, published by Associated Publishers and Authors, Wilmington, Del.

1

Experiencing the Holy Spirit

The large crowd which gathered on the Day of Pentecost was greatly influenced through seeing and hearing the Lord's followers glorifying God in tongues (see Acts 2:5-13). So Peter seized the opportunity to explain that the crucified Lord had risen again in power and was now exalted on high. Death could not hold Him! Moreover, as the living exalted Jesus and source of life, He had poured out the Spirit in this visible and audible way (v. 33). Yet there was urgent need that Peter's convicted hearers repent and be baptized and then they too would receive the gift of the Holy Spirit (2:14-38). And as a result, 3000 people—eager for God and open to the same supernatural coming of the Spirit upon their own lives as they had just observed in the 120—responded and received forgiveness and the gift of the Spirit for themselves.

The order of belief, baptism and reception of the Spirit which Peter mentioned here was probably the usual sequence of events in the early months of the Church's life. Yet Luke, recording under the leading of the Spirit, emphasizes that even as little as two years after Pentecost, this was neither the *only* possible sequence, nor was God's response automatic or inevitable.[1] The Wind would blow where and when it would: Therefore God's people must learn the lesson of constantly looking to and keeping up with the Lord, rather than transferring their trust to any supposedly rigid sequence or theological formula. Like the Israelites, they must accompany the cloud whether it rested in one place or moved on (see Num. 9:18-23).

God's Order Is Flexible

While basic features of repentance/belief, baptism and reception of the Holy Spirit remained constant, *the order* in which these were experienced fluctuated greatly. This variety can be better appreciated if we group together the heart response of repentance and belief in Christ and refer to this experience as 1, to baptism as 2, and reception of the Spirit as 3. This order (1, 2, 3) was mentioned by Peter in his message to the multitude on the Day of Pentecost (Acts 2:37-38), but at Caesarea (10:44-48) the sequence was belief and Holy Spirit apparently simultaneously, followed by baptism (1 & 3, 2). Sometimes, however, in the divine sovereignty or because of some lack in those who received, not only was the *order* changed, but a definite time lapse (—) occurred. The order then became belief, delay, hands, Holy Spirit, baptism (1 — 3, 2) as with Paul (9:1-18); or belief, baptism, delay, hands, Holy Spirit (1, 2 — 3) as with the Smaritans and the Ephesians (8:14-18; 19:1-6).

Thus, even excluding the outpouring upon the 120, there are four major biblical variations, but in all cases, before the total initiation event was completed, belief, baptism and the Spirit were each experienced.

Varying Terms for the Same Supernatural Reality

As for the reception of the Holy Spirit, equivalent terms are used interchangeably. This is clear when we compare the phrases, noting that although different facets are highlighted, it is the same spiritual reality shining through and being described from different vantage points.

The following table sets out the parallel expressions used to describe what took place.

The First Disciples: The Acts 2:1-4 Occasion
   filling with the Spirit (initial fullness—2:4)
   baptized in (or with) the Holy Spirit (1:5)
   a coming upon of the Spirit (1:8; see Luke 24:49)
   a clothing with power from on high (Luke 24:49)
   the promise of the Father (Luke 24:49; see Acts 2:33)
   receiving or taking the Holy Spirit (2:38; 10:47)
   a pouring out of God's Spirit (2:16-18, 33)
   the gift of the Holy Spirit (2:38)

The Samaritans: The Acts 8:14-21 Occasion
   receiving or taking the Holy Spirit (8:15, 17, 19)
   a falling upon of the Spirit (8:16)
   a giving of the Holy Spirit (8:18)
   the gift of God (8:20)

Paul: The Acts 9:10-18 Occasion
   filling with the Spirit (initial fullness—9:17)

Cornelius and Household: The Acts 10:44-48 Occasion

the falling upon of the Spirit (10:44; 11:15)
the gift of the Holy Spirit (10:45; see 11:17; 15:8-9)
the pouring out of the Holy Spirit (10:45)
receiving or taking the Holy Spirit (10:47)
baptized in (or with) the Holy Spirit (11:16)

The Ephesians: The Acts 19:1-7 Occasion
receiving or taking the Holy Spirit (19:2)
a coming upon of the Holy Spirit (19:6)

All these phrases relate to the same spiritual reality and are equivalent ways of describing the same sudden, supernatural coming of the Spirit, "a coming which was such a dramatic and overpowering experience that it almost exhausted Luke's vocabulary to find language which would give an adequate description of its richness and fullness." [2]

We are therefore confining ourselves unnecessarily, and to our loss, if we build our theology of "baptism in the Spirit" on that term alone, while excluding many other ways of describing the identical experience. The initial filling is the baptism in the Spirit, which in turn is the receiving of the Spirit, which is the "falling upon" and the "pouring out" of God's Spirit "which you see and hear." Or, looked at differently, on each person in these groups there was an outpouring, a baptism in the Spirit, an initial filling, a receiving, and so on. This means, for example, that Paul's initial filling can validly be referred to by any of these rich, synonymous expressions found in the book of Acts.

What was God's purpose in introducing the particular concept of *baptism* in the Spirit, and having it recorded repeatedly (Matt. 3:11; Mark 1:8; Luke 3:16; John 1:33; Acts 1:4-5; 11:15-16; 1 Cor. 12:13), when He could have chosen lesser terms such as *having* the Spirit? It is clear that He took up the well-known picture of baptism (*baptisma*, immersion)—associated as it was with entering a new realm—to emphasize the profound and wonderful reality of the Spirit within the believer's life, and to stress a depth and dynamism of spiritual meaning.

To be baptized in the Spirit refers to nothing less than to be immersed, inundated, flooded, invaded and surrounded with the searching and very personal Spirit of God. This was a profound reality that affected a believer's total being and left its mark upon his memory, personality and spirit. [3] No intelligent believer could hear and respond to God's truth and be immersed, inundated or flooded with water in a service of Christian baptism without knowing it, for it was a fully conscious and deeply meaningful act, and it thereafter *remained* as a memorable experience. No one needed to theologize or investigate records to verify whether he had in fact been flooded by water. And when early Christians had been baptized in the Spirit, they did not need to examine texts and precedents or be indoctrinated to know whether they had had a dynamic encounter with Jesus the Baptizer and with the mighty Spirit of God.

Laurie Guy has stated this well: "In the work of the Spirit, being baptized by the Spirit, being born again of the Spirit, and being sanctified by the Spirit are not synonymous terms. Each emphasizes a different facet and this may mean that a man born of the Spirit is not yet baptized in the Spirit. Each term is intended to correspond to reality. Thus it is the nature of the reality which determines which term is used. One may say one is 'baptized in the Spirit' only if one really has had a good bath in the Spirit. God may start a new work in us (regeneration) without giving us that bath. Until such time we are not *baptized* in the Spirit. . . . New Testament words match inward reality. A man is baptized in the Spirit, not when his theology says he is, but when he is actually flooded with God's Spirit. Men of the New Testament had been so flooded with the Spirit that they were indeed '*baptized* in the Holy Spirit.' "[4]

The word "baptism," then, points to a *profound* and *memorable* introduction to a new mode and dimension of living. Initiation and profundity are both present in the term.

Luke most frequently refers to the act of being baptized in the Spirit as "receiving or taking the Holy Spirit" (see Acts 2:38; 8:15, 17, 19; 10:47; 19:2), a term which emphasizes the need for appropriation, for Christians did not speak of *believing* in the Spirit but of *receiving* Him. Wherever *lambanō* (to take, receive) is used in connection with the Spirit, it serves to stress that there was nothing casual, passive or theoretical about this reception, for it involved an active receiving/taking—or, expressed differently, a total openness and eager readiness to receive God's supply. (See some uses of the word in Matt. 10:38; 26:26-27; John 1:12; 10:17-18; 12:48; 20:22; Rev. 22:17.)[5] In illustration of this, Jesus likened the act of receiving the Spirit to that of drinking, for He says: "If any one thirst, let him come to me and *drink*" (John 7:37), and drinking always involves an active process of receiving. It is never a passive or automatic act.

The good news of the Kingdom had been preached and everyone must enter it with hunger, thirst and the violence of desperation (see Isa. 44:3; John 7:37-38; Luke 16:16), eager to meet the conditions and know nothing less than the same quality of life and access to God that the Christians around him were currently enjoying.

Any Deficiency Quickly Remedied

After the descent of the Spirit at Pentecost, belief, baptism and the reception of the Holy Spirit were regarded as basic requirements, and were the experience of all New Testament Christians. These events could occur on the same occasion (Acts 10:44-48), or they could be briefly separated as happened more commonly (Acts 8:14-18; 9:1-18; 19:5-6), but *in each case where they were separated the matter was dealt with urgently. It was never ignored as insignificant or left to correct itself.*

For example, when Peter and John first heard about the obvious deficiency in the baptized believers in Samaria,[6] they did not merely send off a letter to correct or explain the irregularity, or suggest that since they had believed in Jesus Christ they must have received the Holy Spirit, and they should gladly and in faith recognize this! Neither did they send word that they would visit Samaria at a later date and deal with the matter then. Some subjects could well wait and be dealt with during a later visit (see 1 Cor. 11:34), but not this one. So the apostles left immediately, that *at the earliest moment* the lack within the Samaritans could be supplied.

The same urgency was shown with Paul. *As soon as Ananias understood his commission* he went to pray for Paul so that without further delay he could be filled with the Spirit for the first time.

Later, Paul instructed twelve Ephesian believers and saw them accept his teaching and receive full Christian baptism (Acts 19:5). Whatever had been the extent of their spiritual experience before, they had now undoubtedly entered into a living relationship with Christ. Yet in spite of this, Paul would still not leave them until he had convincing evidence that they also had received the Spirit, for this too was a basic part of the gospel, and at that moment it was more important for initiation to be completed than for him to press on with further missionary activity. Neither would he at that time instruct them to keep on being filled with the Spirit, for that would have been quite impossible! There was something even more basic! There had to be an experience of receiving the Spirit before repeated infillings could take place. As it was apparent that these Ephesians had not yet received the initial infilling, Paul would pray for them *immediately*, and not leave them before he had seen the Holy Spirit come upon them.

Spirit Consistently Received by All

It is very clear that if Paul had held some doctrine common today, he would not have addressed the twelve Ephesians as he did, nor acted as promptly. Instead, either when he first met them or after their instruction and Christian baptism, he would have had a conversation somewhat like this:

"Well, now that you are believers in Jesus Christ I have good news for you. Not only have you been forgiven, but the moment you truly believed you received everything, including the Holy Spirit. You were baptized in the Holy Spirit, and now the important thing for you is to realize that you *already* have the Holy Spirit within you. You are complete in Christ, and you need nothing further except to draw by faith on His almighty resources. From now on just trust Him to work."

That may sound reassuring but it contrasts markedly with what Paul said. His conversation was more along the following lines:

"Well, now that you are believers in Jesus Christ I have good news for you. Although you have already been forgiven you should also know that you can receive the Holy Spirit. This can occur either when or after people believe in Christ.[7] Have you therefore personally *received* the Holy Spirit?"

"No!," they answered, "we have never heard that the Holy Spirit has been given."[8]

"You have already been baptized in a baptism of repentance administered by John the Baptist. Since you now believe in Jesus Christ who has died, has risen, has been glorified, and has poured forth the Holy Spirit as was promised, complete your Christian initiation by taking the next steps of being baptized in water and receiving the Holy Spirit."

On hearing this they were baptized in the name of the Lord Jesus. And when Paul had laid his hands upon them the Holy Spirit came on them; and they spoke with tongues and prophesied (see Acts 19:2-6).

It is clear that even where full apostolic instruction had been given and Christian baptism administered, the Holy Spirit was not necessarily received. And when this could be so, there is obviously no basis for the view that regular modern instruction and baptism today will always confer what was not always conferred in the New Testament Church—even when apostles were involved.

For their part, Christian leaders had an immediate duty to ensure that all believers received the total experience of the Spirit. Though, as we have seen, there might be a short delay, all must experience belief, baptism, and the Holy Spirit before the new Christian's initiation was complete. Yet rather than being considered as three separate events, they were regarded as different aspects of the single event of becoming a Christian. The Church certainly did not permit three classes of Christians—believing Christians; believing and baptized Christians; and believing, baptized and Spirit-filled Christians. Where there was any deficiency, the Church acted immediately to make certain they *all* became the latter, who then needed to let the Holy Spirit repeatedly fill them. This was normal Christianity (see 1 Cor. 12:13).[9]

Observable Reception

The question never arose as to whether a believer was a Christian without baptism, and the New Testament writers did not therefore write or construct their theology with unbaptized Christians in mind,[10] for such would be a contradiction and an exercise in futility. Yet equally, they did not regard a believer as fully initiated into the Christian life and the redeemed community unless he had received the Spirit in an unmistakable fashion, for that would have been equally contradictory.

This explains why after Pentecost there are no written commands for believers to receive the Spirit initially. They had already done so. It was the norm to receive Him immediately in a vivid, concrete way, and if there was any glaring departure from this, it was promptly rectified, not by commands in letters, but by more immediate personal intervention and prayer. Though all believers in the early Church were baptized and received the Spirit, in most cases neither their water baptism nor reception of the Spirit was recorded, for these events had become commonplace and the established pattern, and as such they no longer needed restating.[11] Yet in every case where the Spirit's initial reception *is* actually described, His coming was accompanied by definite supernatural manifestations of His gracious presence. What is more, this natural activity of the Spirit caused not the slightest surprise! There was surprise only when the Spirit's customary activity was *not* immediately obvious.

When early Christians received the promise of the Spirit

through faith (see Gal. 3:14), they received the *fullness* of the promise, and certainly there was no thought given to the concept, current today in some quarters, of gradually maturing into a state of fullness. Neither was there thought of an immersion in the Spirit which took place more or less automatically, inevitably, unconsciously and invisibly upon their belief or belief and baptism.

A Closer Study of an Important Text

Paul's statement that "Any one who does not have the Spirit of Christ does not belong to him" (Rom. 8:9) is often said to teach that if you are a Christian you have the Spirit.[12] That could well be regarded as a valid deduction from Paul's words, but it does in fact *reverse* the particular point he was making. He was rather *arguing from possession or absence of the Spirit* as to whether a person was a Christian—not vice versa. This is an important distinction. Not, "I am a Christian, so I know I must have the Spirit," but, "I have the Spirit (given as God's response to my obedience of faith); so God has accepted me. I am therefore a Christian." Conversely, "If I do not have the Spirit I am not a Christian. God has not accepted me." Paul could reason this way (in a situation very different from the general pattern prevailing today) because possession of the Spirit was then a fact of immediate perception and experience, and His absence was conspicuous.

Acts and the epistles bear this same testimony. For example, we are specifically shown that the Spirit was perceived and experienced by the 120 at Jerusalem (Acts 2:1-12), by many early Christians (Acts 4:29-31), Stephen (Acts 6:8, 7:55), Paul (e.g., Acts 9:17-18; 13:9-12), Timothy (1 Tim. 1:18; 4:14-15; 2 Tim. 1:6), Titus (Titus 3:5-6); at Samaria (Acts 8:14-19), Caesarea (Acts 10:27, 44-48), Ephesus (Acts 19:1-7 with Eph. 1:13; 1 Cor. 16:8 with 14:18-19), Thessalonica (1 Thess. 1:6; 5:19-20), Corinth (e.g., 1 Cor. 1:4-7; 2:12-14), in Galatia (Gal. 3:2-5), at Rome (e.g., Rom. 1:11-12; 5:5; 8:9, 14, 26-27), and, as we shall now see, wherever there were Christians.

In commenting on the phrase, "Any one who does not have the Spirit of Christ does not belong to him" (Rom. 8:9), C. H. Dodd says, "Paul could with confidence write in such terms . . . for *it was the universal assumption of primitive Christianity, attested by all parts of the New Testament, that when a man came to Christ he received a supernatural gift of divine power; and this assumption must have corresponded with general experience.*" [13] [14] This was such a universal pattern that Paul knew it was true even in a distant Roman congregation which he had not, at that time, visited. It was true everywhere!

When Cornelius and his family and friends spoke in tongues and magnified God, such a power to offer up supernatural worship immediately convinced the early Church that upon people who were not Christians before, "the gift of the Holy Spirit had been poured out." They had now "received the Holy Spirit." And because God had given such evidence of His acceptance, as all could see, these people were now entitled to be accepted as Christians and baptized in water (See Acts 10:45-47). Such a pattern exactly parallels the direction of Paul's thought within Rom. 8:9, for in both instances the argument proceeds from the supernatural evidence, to the spiritual reality itself.

James Dunn sums up what many have noticed throughout the pages of the New Testament: "The reception of the Spirit in New Testament days was an event of which recipient and onlooker could not but be aware. . . . The vivid experience of receiving the Spirit . . . and the effect of His coming . . . is ever to the forefront of Paul's thought."[15]

Paul himself had become fully regenerate before his encounter with Ananias.[16] But although this was so, it was not until three days later that he received the Spirit and was baptized. Similarly, although the Samaritans and the Ephesians had genuinely believed in Christ, their initial response was not complete in itself but led on to a further important and obvious experience of the Spirit.

The Spirit of God moved upon different people in different sequences, but whether simultaneously with belief, or subsequently, He brought them to the same anchorage in Christ and to the same observable reception of the Spirit.

The Same Reality Required Today

Although the early Christians were immersed in the Spirit, it is quite unrealistic to assert that all twentieth-century believers have also experienced the same. That no more follows than saying because all New Testament believers had been immersed in water soon after they turned to the Lord, all present-day believers have also had this experience. It is self-evident, however, that what was true of them is not necessarily true of all believers today: it would only be true of a church which was as keen as Peter and John, Ananias and Paul to see that all believers have been fully initiated. But today not only have many believers had no one minister to them, if need be with laying on of hands, but they have been actively warned against pursuing the matter further. This frequently creates a fundamental difference between early Church and modern experience.

Thomas Smail makes this same point when he writes: "The whole question of the actual level of the Church's spiritual experience and why it has fallen so woefully short of the experience of the first Church, cannot be swept under the carpet by claiming that in the theology of the New Testament there is an essential connection between baptism and Pentecost.

"To address the contemporary Church as if every statement made about the Church in scripture were automatically true of it, quite apart from its present state and condition, to tell believers who know themselves to be spiritually inadequate that rivers of living water are pouring from them, to tell those who feel futile and fruitless in their Christian service that the outpoured energy of the Holy Spirit is freely at work in them, to tell Christians who are hardly aware of the Holy Spirit that they are already baptized in the Spirit, solely because the New Testament is interpreted as saying that all Christians are baptized in the Spirit—all this is to run into complete unreality. The New Testament speaks of people being full of the Spirit, or of the Church being baptized in the Spirit, in the light of the actual experience of the churches and people to whom these words were addressed, and they can be applied with reality only to people who have had the same thing happen to them."[17]

Many Christians have genuinely believed in the Lord Jesus Christ and been baptized, but their experience has stopped short of that which the New Testament describes and God intends. What God has joined together has all too frequently been allowed to drift apart, with the result that vast numbers have not entered into the fullness of their inheritance.

Frequently believers are taught that, through believing in Christ, they have received all God wishes to give them, and so they become satisfied and complacent with a pre-pentecostal experience of the Spirit. Undoubtedly they enjoy spiritual life, but they have not received the promise of the Father. They have not been baptized in the Spirit and their initial development is therefore incomplete. However, God wants them to know the *fullness* of His New Covenant provision: repentance, belief in Christ, baptism, and baptism in the Spirit, followed by a life which is open to His repeated infilling.

Yet what does it mean to believe in Christ? For it obviously means much more than to make a decision to accept Him. Thomas

Smail has stated it thus: "Christ is the ultimate object of every scriptural promise and . . . we find every spiritual blessing in Him. It is true that if we believe in Christ we do not have to believe in anything else.

"But we also need to be clear that the Christ in whom we believe is not a Christ restricted to that area of operation which our own particular brand of Christian tradition allots to Him, but rather the whole Christ in the whole range and extent of His Person and Work and of the gospel's offer to us. We have in fact to relate ourselves in faith to the one who is everything indicated by His name, Jesus, Lord, and Christ, who operates on the comprehensive scale indicated in the New Testament, who is therefore not only the lamb of God who takes away the sin of the world but also He who will baptize us with the Holy Spirit and with fire." [18]

The Way Forward

Today, any lack we have lies not in the realm of God's giving, but in our desire, faith, openness and receptivity to Christ and the Spirit He bestows. Convinced that there was no lack from God's side, Paul did not ask, *"Did God give you the Holy Spirit when you believed?"*, but *"Did you receive or take the Holy Spirit when you believed?"* (Acts 19:2). (Similarly, we note in John 12:48 that Jesus' words were given but were not automatically taken.)

God unquestionably adjusts His giving to our taking. If we earnestly desire the Spirit with manifestations of His love and grace, we *receive* the Spirit with His 'Spirit-natural' manifestations. Conversely, if we claim to be open to the Spirit yet remain suspicious of His supernatural workings, we minimize our ability to receive His fullness. We have erected a barrier of unbelief which God will not forcibly remove. He waits to see if we will respond to further enlightenment from the Spirit and begin to thirst for fullness on His terms. If we do, He is able to lead us into further enrichment.

The Lord may not answer a Christian's prayer for fullness with accompanying gifts until He has dealt with any hindrance of pride in relationship to others in the Body of Christ (see 1 Cor. 12:14-26). He wants to do far more than fill individuals with His Spirit, wonderful though that is. He wants to correct any tendency to live independently, especially in those who find it difficult to submit to prayer and laying on of hands from another member of the Body. God frequently meets a person without laying on of hands (Acts 2:1-4; 10:44-48), but He has chosen that others meet Him in this way (Acts 8:15-18; 9:17-18; 19:6; Heb. 6:1-2 [19]). Through laying on of hands by someone in touch with God He may minister to a proud and independent spirit, or bring needful reassurance or teaching to some unsure child of God. But whether the reality occurs when the believer is alone or when prayed for by another, God's purpose is for His Spirit to fill completely, giving the same release of spiritual gifts which was normal in the early Church.

Each generation, and every individual within that generation needs a personal relationship with Jesus for salvation. Similarly, each Christian needs to be filled with the Holy Spirit with His accompanying gifts, for nobody can be borne along by any spiritual impetus that some earlier generation has experienced. They must receive for themselves.

Biblical theology will always be important. Yet we do well to remind ourselves that in the first Church the *fact* of the Spirit's blessing and reality came before the full theological understanding of it. Their experience of God was their starting-point. This awareness will protect us from any modern theories or doctrines that effectively leave us with less than the early Christians experienced.

These days we must remain receptive lest we miss what God is saying and doing by His Spirit. And if we want the full blessing of God himself—without reservations in our spirit—call it what we will, He will answer the prayer of the thirsty heart even if our theological terminology lacks precision (see Matt. 5:3, 6; Isa. 41:17; 43:19-21; 44:3-4).

At the earliest possible moment God desires our total lives to be bathed in the presence, grace and power of His Spirit. Whether this takes one, two, or more steps, and however it may be described, the Lord desires to bring us into a spiritual reality where we may enjoy and effectively express Christ's love in action. This is our privilege and responsibility. God's promise, "You will seek Me and find Me, when you search for Me with all your heart. And I will be found by you . . . ," still presents a fundamental biblical principle (Jer. 29:13-14, NASB).

And when we have received enrichment by His Spirit, it is not because of merit or our standing before Him, but solely because God is gracious. Through His undeserved favor we are better able to worship and serve Him than we were before.

2

Initiation in a Modern Setting

There are some important aspects of our subject which require additional attention before we proceed, and these we shall consider in turn.

Can Baptized Believers Be Without the Spirit?

Many modern Christians are sensitive about affirming that baptized believers can be without the Holy Spirit. The participators in New Testament history such as Peter, John, Philip, Paul and Luke (and no doubt all the others) did not share this concern. These leaders recognized that believers could be without the Spirit and they had no hesitation about saying so (Acts 8:4-19; 19:1-7; see Luke 11:5-13; Matt. 7:11), though when this happened it was urgently rectified. They realized that there would be a short process of transition from the state of being untouched by the gospel until initiation into the Christian life was complete. During that time a person heard the Word, accepted it intellectually, seriously faced the requirement of making Jesus Lord and taking up the cross, repented, inwardly responded in faith, made known his decision to follow Christ, waited, however briefly, while representatives of the church arranged the time and place for his baptism, submitted to baptism and was filled with the Spirit with an acceptable supernatural manifestation. Theologically, these were joined in the one initiatory event of becoming a Christian, but in the experience of the convert they were necessarily separated by a short space of time.[1]

The apostles did not debate the precise moment when a person became a "Christian" and a member of God's family. They were more interested in bringing him promptly to full Christian experience. Then when *all* these aspects had been fulfilled, he was unquestionably a Christian. The apostles were convinced that these constituted the essential foundation for balance and continuing growth into full maturity. Paul could therefore write to the Christian churches in the certainty that the customary requirements had been fulfilled, the transition was past, and all did indeed possess the Spirit.

It would be wrong to imply that a believer had not passed from death to life if he was not baptized in water or had not received the Spirit with accompanying signs. The Old Testament saints and the repentant thief received eternal life without either. But it is equally wrong to imply that our Lord and His apostles would be content with Christian initiation unless those in the new and greater age of the Spirit (see 2 Cor. 3:7-11; Heb. 8-10) had individually experienced all these aspects.

No Manifestations, Thank You!

No one can validly say, "I believe I have been baptized in the Holy Spirit, but I want no supernatural manifestations."

To be satisfied with some initial filling with the Spirit (that is baptism in the Spirit) which allows no place for its New Testament accompaniments is as contradictory as having a baptism devoid of water, the Lord's Supper without the bread and the cup, or a doctrine of the Body of Christ that allowed no place for the varied functions of its members. But God would not give His Church these outward expressions if there was no spiritual value in exercising them. To be content without the experience of the gifts is to be content with impoverishment or short rations. Blessing may undoubtedly result, but full-orbed spiritual reality and balance cannot be realized.

God wants us to develop in all areas of spiritual life, not just in some of them. In the life of the early Church the fact of receiving the Spirit was so interwoven with the outward accompaniments that they could not be separated without emasculating biblical doctrine and diminishing Christian experience.

The Accompanying and Indwelling Spirit

We have already seen that when believers received the Spirit there were obvious and supernatural signs of His presence, and that this became such a universal pattern that the Church could argue from it as to who did and did not belong to God. It is therefore relatively easy to understand Rom. 8:9 in the context of New Testament Christianity, where the Spirit came immediately, or, if not, where the Church intervened and cooperated with the Lord to see that the Spirit's temporary absence never became permanent. It is not, however, so easy to apply this verse to today's situation where there has been a widespread departure from the New Testament pattern of initiation. In other words, the suit that perfectly fitted Paul's Spirit-baptized man does not fit a modern Christian, unless he, like his New Testament counterpart, has been baptized in water and in the Spirit, and evidences this latter baptism by the same supernatural accompaniments.

How then can we relate Paul's words to today's anomalous situation, where many believers have inherited an incomplete initiation system that bears little resemblance to the richness of early practice and experience? How do we understand the believer's relationship to the Spirit prior to his Spirit baptism, where, contrary to the New Testament pattern, faith, baptism and Spirit baptism have been generally allowed to remain separate one from the other, or where there is no place for baptism or Spirit baptism at all? This is a question that would not have concerned early Christians because the transitional stage between their conversion and Spirit baptism was so short. However, it is a question we are forced to consider.

The following alternatives represent the two major lines of thought:

1. Some appeal to the experience of the Lord's disciples prior to Pentecost. On the first Easter Day Jesus had breathed upon them and said, "Receive the Holy Spirit" (John 20:22). At this point with the incoming of the Holy Spirit, the disciples, it is argued, received the breath of new life. They now had the life of God within them, and with this they entered into a new depth of relationship with Jesus and a greater authority than they had before (v. 23). Yet this did not make superfluous their later pentecostal baptism in the Spirit in which He came in fullness with other gifts and a greater purpose.

Those who see this as an analogy say that upon belief Jesus breathes the Spirit of life into believers. They then have the Spirit, are born of the Spirit, and are saved. The fact that the Church could say baptized believers had *not* yet received the Spirit is understood to mean they had not received the Spirit in the way defined in Acts 8:16—that is, He had not yet fallen upon (*epi*) any of them. Then after being prayed for they received the outpouring of the Spirit in the regular pentecostal way.

This is an attractive suggestion but it has serious weaknesses. (a) The apostles were already regenerate and had divine life within them not only prior to Pentecost but prior to the inbreathing of John 20:22 (see Matt. 19:27; Luke 9:1-2; 10:17 with 11:20; John

13:10-11; 14:17; 15:3-11, 19; 17:9-10, 14-16; 17:6 with 1 John 3:24; John 16:27 and 17:8 with 1 John 5:1; John 20:17). Equally, the Old Testament saints, the seventy and the repentant thief knew nothing of this inbreathing, yet were regenerate without it (Luke 10:20; 23:42-43). (b) After Pentecost the Church could state without any qualification that there were baptized believers in Christ who had *not* received the Spirit (Acts 8:14-18; 19:5-6; see 9:1-18). (c) Where belief and Spirit baptism were briefly separated, there is no indication of a double reception of the Spirit, once silently when they believed and the next time with pentecostal manifestations.

2. A better explanation is that the Spirit dwells *with* the born-again believer in Christ, but does not indwell him until he receives or is baptized in the Spirit. This is in line with the distinction Jesus made when He said, "He dwells with you and will be in you" (John 14:17).[2] The Spirit can be at work in a person's life and bring him to faith without residing within that life. We have already seen how the apostles and others had been won to Christ and regenerated prior to the inbreathing of John 20:22 (see also John 3:3-8; 16:8-11; Acts 7:51).

Borrowing the language of Rom. 8:9, we could say that a Christian "has" the Holy Spirit accompanying or dwelling with him to convict, awaken faith, reveal Christ, and bring him to new birth. However, the fact that these have occurred is not by itself evidence that the Spirit dwells *in* that person. Then when he is baptized in the Spirit the Spirit who was present *with* him becomes, in addition, also resident *within* him. He has been received or taken into the believer's life.

Unlike the former, this latter view does not require us to read into Luke's history of the Church a silent receiving of the Spirit of which there is no hint within Acts, indeed, which is at variance with its testimony. The latter interpretation makes no recourse to John 20:22, for this is seen as a definite but interim receiving of the Spirit by the disciples prior to Pentecost, but which was superseded later by the Spirit's descent.

To be true to the original meaning of Rom. 8:9, we dare not ignore the fact that when Paul said, "Any one who does not have the Spirit of Christ does not belong to him," the starting point of his argument was based not on any profession, commitment or invisible presence, but on the supernatural and observable experience of the Spirit in the believer's life, and by which his relationship with Christ was manifest (see also Acts 10:45-47;

2 Cor. 1:22; Gal. 3:2-5; Eph. 1:13; Titus 3:5-6; etc.).[3] Paul's original readers would, therefore, understand his words in this strong sense.

Today, however, many believers have had no such experience. They live in an anomalous situation where the original united initiatory process, as seen in the New Testament, has been split and usually left incomplete. The obvious and accepted signs of the Spirit's incoming—which Paul took for granted—are frequently conspicuous by their absence. In such circumstances Rom. 8:9 is not strictly applicable, for it assumes the universality of a different spiritual dimension, upon which Paul built his argument. Today there are many who know little of the Spirit's reality, although they may know the doctrine. They have experienced a genuine pre-pentecostal work of the Spirit, as in John 14:17, but have made the mistake of believing that because they know they have been born again this must have been their Pentecost.

As we have already noted, in the early Church Spirit baptism with its associated indwelling and infilling could occur on the same occasion (Acts 10:44-48), or, more commonly, quickly follow belief in Christ (Acts 8:14-18; 9:1-18; 19:1-7). There was therefore only the briefest time lapse, if any, for the Spirit to be dwelling *with*, rather than *in*, the believer. Believers today who are equally open to the Lord can also receive with the minimum of delay, and should be eager to do so.

We can therefore make these brief points in summary:

(1) There can be no relationship with Christ apart from the Spirit's activity.

(2) People today who have been born of the Spirit are regenerate and have the Spirit with them.

(3) Because the early Church never permitted initiation to remain incomplete, Christians in New Testament times had the Spirit not only *with* them but *in* them.

(4) None of these statements, although true, expresses the underlying assumption of Paul's argument in Rom. 8:9, for he assumed that the Spirit's presence was universally and outwardly marked by a dynamic supernatural gift. From this he then argued as to whether a person belonged to Christ: that is, he argued from the outward supernatural evidence to the inward reality. This verse, therefore, refutes any view of a silent, unnoticed "theological" presence of the Spirit.

(5) If we have not this same demonstrable and supernatural verification that was universally enjoyed in the early Church,

we can respond to the Lord and quickly receive the Spirit with this same supernatural evidence.

Attitudes

Whatever our experience has been, we should not forget that it is only the grace of God which has brought us this far. The one who has progressed less distance in one area may have progressed much further in others, or be progressing faster. There is therefore no room for arrogance on one side, or hurt feelings on the other. If we are Christ's, whether initially filled with the Spirit or not, we have the privilege of fellowshipping as brothers. (See commentary on 1 Cor. 13:4-8a in the author's book, *Love and Gifts.*)

Yet while attitudes must be right, we must also recognize and recover the dynamic New Testament experience of the Spirit, rather than allow its message and relevance to be toned down. Regardless of what others do and think, we personally must not be lulled into accepting for ourselves any current practice and standard of life that is less than its New Testament counterpart. If we have not been baptized in the Spirit, we should earnestly seek to enter by the grace of God into the fullness of which the New Testament speaks. And those of us who have already entered should walk in love and go on to maturity lest we be quickly overtaken by the godly enthusiasm and dedication of those who began after us!

Modern Christians who have been baptized in the Spirit a long time after their conversion, usually think of themselves as very belatedly coming into that which ideally should have been linked closely with their initial belief and Christian baptism. Where this delay has occurred it is understandable that Holy Spirit baptism is often regarded as a second stage—or even a third stage if baptism in water took place well after conversion—but it would be more correct to regard it as the belated completion of their initiation. It is enthusiastically agreed that it would be much better and more in accord with Bible practice if this event had been linked closely with their belief and baptism, but it is better that it occur later than not at all! Although late, at least there is a return to full biblical experience! (It would of course be much better still, and reduce any delay, if the Church had more Peters and Johns, Ananiases, Lukes and Pauls, who would insist that we quickly receive the full initiatory experience of the Spirit!)

Christians who respond to Jesus the Baptizer in this way are not trying to demonstrate that they are better than others who see no need for anything further in their Christian life. For themselves, however, they are unimpressed with any merely symbolic, theological or dry "immersion" or "flooding" in the Spirit. They want instead the knowable, verifiable objective experience of the Spirit: the pentecostal reality portrayed in the Bible.

This objective experience of Christ and the Holy Spirit is sought and found not to separate us from other Christians but to unite ourselves as best we can with the will of God and the experience of the early Christians. Then, having had the initial experience of the Spirit as they had, we need like them to continue to grow to know the Lord better and to live and walk in the Spirit. We have by no means "arrived" but have experienced a glorious beginning of life in a previously unencountered dimension, and are very aware that we are only learners, children in God's school. There are two ideas we want to express together. We want with Paul to say:

> Blessed be the God and Father of our Lord Jesus Christ who has blessed us in Christ with every spiritual blessing. . . . In him we have redemption through his blood, the forgiveness of our trespasses, according to the riches of his grace which he lavished upon us (Eph. 1:3, 7),

and, mindful of how much more there is in God, to also add:

> Not that I have already obtained . . . or am already perfect; but . . . I press on toward the goal for the prize of the upward call of God in Christ Jesus (Phil. 3:12, 14).

3

Fullness and Gifts

Every Christian is commanded to be filled with the Spirit (Eph. 5:18). This is therefore God's will for all believers.

Yet what does it mean to be filled with the Spirit and what happens when a person is filled?

There are many terms used in Scripture to indicate various aspects of the life of the believer—such as justification, being born of the Spirit, sanctification of the Spirit, fruit of the Spirit—and each of these has its own particular significance and its own association of ideas. Naturally these terms may in a measure overlap, for there is an interrelationship between all aspects of the Christian life. Yet each term carries its own distinctive emphasis, and to be properly understood, must be considered separately. Thus, for example, baptism gathers around itself ideas of witness, death, burial, resurrection, change of ownership, entrance into the Church, and so on. The fullness of the Spirit does the same, and concerns a distinctive facet of the Spirit's ministry.

Distinctly Supernatural

When we analyze the occurrences of the expressions "filled with the Spirit" and "full of the Spirit," we see how fullness was accompanied by certain consequences. It had a very practical and immediate outcome. Fullness referred not to some undefined or nebulous spiritual state, but to a specific and definite enabling given by the Holy Spirit. *When a person was filled with the Spirit, he received supernatural inspiration and illumination, and power to worship and to serve God and men effectively.* It was not that human abilities were trained or enhanced (though this may well have been a not unnatural outcome), but that the Holy Spirit gave distinctly supernatural powers for the supernatural accomplishment of a task, or to supply an individual's need.

Notice how the purpose and the consequences of the Spirit's full-ness stand out in the accounts that follow. It will be seen how the Wind of God comes in its (His) fullness to give new ways of think-ing, acting, serving and worshipping.

Early in the Old Testament people were filled with the Spir-it and received a divine impartation of wisdom and ability which enabled them to do what was otherwise quite beyond their human capacity. "The Lord said . . . , 'I have filled him [Be-zalel] with the Spirit of God, with ability and intelligence, with knowledge and all craftsmanship, to devise . . . , to work . . . ' " (Ex. 31:3-4; 35:30-35). Later we read that Joshua was full of the spirit [or Spirit] of wisdom, for Moses had laid his hands upon him" (Deut. 34:9).

The term "filled with the Spirit" is used of the infant John the Baptist who was specially set apart for his future ministry as a prophet of the Lord (Luke 1:15-17). His would be a supernaturally guided life and an equipped ministry. He would drink no wine nor strong drink, and through being filled with the Holy Spirit he would receive the necessary inspiration, guidance and strength for the fulfillment of his unique prophetic calling. God would have His hand on him from birth, in divine preparation for his singular min-istry of preparing for the Messiah.

When Elizabeth was filled with the Spirit she spoke prophet-ically words she could confidently know only by divine inspira-tion: "Blessed are you among women, and blessed is the fruit of your womb! And why is this granted me, that the mother of my Lord should come to me? . . ." With the fullness came a super-natural working of the Spirit within her body as her baby leaped to acknowledge the presence of the Son of God. In this case the timing plus the movement was the evidence of supernatural inter-vention (Luke 1:41-45).

Zechariah was filled with the Holy Spirit and immediately prophesied, again, like Elizabeth, expressing thoughts that were known only because God had spoken (Luke 1:67-79).

When our Lord was filled with the Holy Spirit, the Spirit minis-tered to Him supernaturally and specially equipped Him for future ministry. He received a vision of the opened heaven, He saw the Holy Spirit descend upon Him in bodily form as a dove, and He heard a message direct from the Father which confirmed His unique Sonship. After this He is described as being "full of the Holy Spirit" (see Luke 3:21-22; 4:1). He was then led by the Spirit into the wilderness where it became evident that He had received supernatural resources to fight the power of Satan. He was being supplied with the Spirit's supernatural power to fight evil in the service of God and men.

On the Day of Pentecost when the 120 were filled with the Spirit, they suddenly received the ability to worship God in tongues (Acts 2:4-11).

Later, following the healing of the lame man, Peter who had been one of the 120, was again filled with the Spirit when the rulers and elders demanded he explain what had happened and the source of the power he and John exercised. With the infilling came immediate strength and inspiration to witness fearlessly, even when Peter and John's lives were threatened by their identification with Him (Acts 4:8-13; see Matt. 10:19-20).

A little later the gathered disciples were filled with the Spirit yet again so that they could overcome the attacks of their opponents. Their prayer for boldness and signs and wonders brought an immediate response. Power was released, and they moved out, proclaiming the Lord Jesus freely and with authority, and with further miraculous evidence as God answered their petition. The shaking of the house they were in and the power they received to speak boldly God's message were closely linked with their infilling (see Acts 4:29-31).

When Stephen was filled with the Spirit, he saw a vision of an open heaven revealing the glory of God, and Jesus standing at His right hand (Acts 7:55-56; see also 6:5, 8).

Paul was instantly healed of blindness and filled with the Spirit when Ananias laid hands upon him (Acts 9:17-18). Though the scripture is silent as to whether this was the time Paul first spoke in tongues, the interrelationship between this and other passages makes it almost certain that he did.[1]

When a false prophet opposed the work of the gospel, Paul was filled with the Spirit and given supernatural ability to exercise three spiritual gifts in succession—discernment of spirits, word of knowledge, and the working of a miracle (Acts 13:9-11).

Paul instructs the Ephesians to "understand what the will of the Lord is," and he immediately follows this with the command to be filled with the Spirit, as though both thoughts were closely related in his mind. He then links this filling with ministry to one another and to the Lord (Eph. 5:17-20).

The concept inherent in "addressing one another" and worshipping the Lord together is the same as Paul mentions in 1 Corinthians (12:7-27; 14:26), where ministering to the Lord and to one an-

other for the upbuilding of every believer, is described in the in-
spirational context of the various gifts and ministries that Christians exercised among themselves. This "Body ministry" with its
singing of songs the Spirit inspired and the offering up of acceptable, heartfelt and joyous praise and thanksgiving to the Lord is
made possible by, and linked closely with, the fullness of the Spirit.

To this evidence above we can add more, for as we saw in the
first chapter, initial fullness is described under other figures of
speech. For example, when the Samaritans, Cornelius, his household and the Ephesians were baptized in the Spirit (that is, initially filled with the Spirit), they too were inspired to manifest obvious
supernatural gifts.

All these passages demonstrate that fullness of the Spirit is associated primarily with inspired worship, inspired revelation, and
inspired service. It is closely associated with divinely given and
extraordinary boldness, varying signs and wonders, tongues,
prophecy, visions, healings, discernment of spirits, words of knowledge, and working of miracles—in other words, with gifts of the
Spirit. It is always directly related to the release of ministry to
the Lord, or, in His name, to men.[2]

A study of these occasions makes it clear that we have correctly
understood God's mind when we see the term "filling with the Spirit" as *synonymous with being under the immediate and powerful
inspiration of the Spirit*. The words are virtually interchangeable.
For the term "filled with the Spirit" we can substitute words such
as "inspired or supernaturally enabled by the Spirit"; and for the
expression "full of the Spirit" the words "open to the inspiration
of the Spirit," without in any way altering the meaning of the passage. This is because *the fullness of the Spirit is itself a reference
to fullness of inspiration (pneuma)*, as God the Holy Spirit breathes
into us His divine energy, enabling, or knowledge. It implies being
sufficiently open to the Lord that direct insight and power are received from Him to minister the gifts of the Spirit effectively. The
realm of fullness is the realm of the obviously supernatural. For
example, we have the correct sense if we paraphrase Acts 2:4:
"The 120 were all inspired by the Holy Spirit (or filled with the
Spirit's inspiration) and began to speak in other tongues."

When relating Simeon's place in bearing witness to Jesus, Luke
had the choice of saying that he was filled with the Spirit, or that
he was "in [or inspired by] the Spirit" (*en tō pneumati*). As a
result Simeon was directed to the temple at the right moment, to
the right infant, and then revealed what God had given him supernaturally. A comparison between Zechariah's filling with the Spirit

and Simeon's being "inspired by the Spirit" shows that these are fully synonymous expressions (Luke 1:67-79; 2:25-35; see also Mark 12:36; Rev. 1:10).

Paul commands his readers: "Do not get drunk with wine, for that is debauchery; but be filled with the Spirit, addressing one another in psalms and hymns and spiritual songs, singing and making melody to the Lord with all your heart, always and for everything giving thanks in the name of our Lord Jesus Christ to God the Father" (Eph. 5:18-20).

Paul is saying: "Live all the time under the direct impulse and enabling of the Spirit, open to His constant inspiration. Make this your *way* of life. Wine would provide a purely human stimulant and dull sensitivity to God's voice. Rather let the Holy Spirit inspire and enable you. You will then be equipped to serve Him in joyous worship and service. Encourage and build up one another by singing psalms and hymns and spiritual songs. Make melody with all your heart as you worship the Lord. And do this in an attitude of interdependence and submission to the ministry of others. Remember, of course, that no inspiration the Lord gives is an end in itself and unrelated to daily living: it is to enable you all to minister acceptably for the enrichment of others, and to serve and worship the Lord in a way the Spirit has himself inspired."

Fullness, then, is linked with manifestations of the Spirit.

The Initial Infilling

Christians are to be repeatedly or continuously filled with the Spirit, as the tense of the verb makes clear. Yet *before anyone can "keep on being filled" he must start with being initially filled.* (In apostolic times this initial fullness was either coincident with saving faith, or very closely linked with it, as mentioned earlier.) Since the descent of the Spirit at Pentecost this initial filling was linked with supernatural manifestations (see Acts 2:4; 8:14-18; 10:44-48; 19:1-6).

Like salvation, fullness was not a theological deduction drawn from scripture: it was a definite experience, though solidly and theologically based. Neither was fullness a reward for living a holy life. Nor, contrary to much modern thought, was it something the early Christians would gradually grow into through the years. People were obviously unfilled and untouched by the Spirit one moment, yet moments later, as they experienced His moving, they were spoken of as "filled with the Spirit" (Acts 2:4; 4:8, 31; 7:55; 13:9; Luke 1:67; see Acts 9:17-18).

The initial filling with the Spirit was a definite experience of divine enabling, given sovereignly to each new Christian either directly or through a member of Christ's Body, to equip him to worship God and to serve both God and men acceptably. Then having been filled at a particular moment, he was to remain receptive to further inspiration and enabling, that is, to a constant state of fullness. The channel must always remain open.

We all need to be filled with the Spirit initially, and then repeatedly. The Lord can then receive the acceptable and inspired worship and service due to Him; we ourselves can worship Him in spirit and in truth and grow in sensitivity and effectiveness; and others can have their needs met more adequately by the illumined Word, specific revelation, and the power of the unchanging Christ (see Heb. 13:8).

4

Holiness and the Fruit of the Spirit

The Lord's followers are called to be consecrated and holy in life and character. We cannot accept the call to follow a perfect Lord yet continue to walk in sin. Habakkuk says of Him: "Thou . . . art of purer eyes than to behold evil, and canst not look on wrong" (Hab. 1:13). God loves us, but in no way can He gloss over sin. If we wish to have fellowship with Him we must be pure in thought, word and deed. Only "he who has clean hands and a pure heart" shall ascend the hill of the Lord and stand in His holy place (Ps. 24:3-6).

Reactions to God's Holy Presence

Yet we face the sad reality that we are sinful and "fall short of the divine splendour" (Rom. 3:23, NEB). Those who have seen a revelation of this aspect of God's person have been instantly overwhelmed by His purity and holiness in stark contrast with their sinfulness. When Isaiah saw the Lord and heard the voice of the seraphim saying "Holy, holy, holy is the Lord of hosts. . . ," his reaction was immediate: "Woe is me! For I am lost; for I am a man of unclean lips" (Isa. 6:5). Job exclaimed: "I had heard of thee by the hearing of the ear, but now my eye sees thee; therefore I despise myself, and repent in dust and ashes" (Job 42:5-6).

While in a boat on the Sea of Galilee Jesus revealed His unique glory, authority and power as He miraculously brought about a huge catch of fish. In awe Peter cried out, "Depart from me, for I am a sinful man, O Lord" (Luke 5:8). Such an unveiling of the Lord's majesty immediately brought painful self-revelation. He felt unworthy in the company of the Holy One of God. Similarly, when John on Patmos saw the splendor of the risen Christ, he "fell at his feet as though dead" (Rev. 1:17). Before this, Ezekiel had seen a vision of God (Ezek. 1:1, 26-27) and declared, "Like a rainbow in the clouds on a rainy day was the sight of that encircling radiance; it was like the appearance of the glory of the Lord, (and) when I saw this I threw myself on my face" (Ezek. 1:28-2:1, NEB; see 1 Kings 8:11).

Self-Centered or God-Centered?

There is only one solution when we realize we have fallen short of God's splendor. Because Jesus willingly offered himself as a perfect sacrifice for our sin, He opened the way for us to be saved and come into line with His will. God alone can justify the ungodly (Rom. 4:5). But before this can happen we must face some imperatives:

"Unless you repent," said Jesus, "you will all perish" (Luke 13:3).

"Unless one is born anew [or from above], he cannot see the kingdom of God" (John 3:3).

"Unless your righteousness exceeds that of the scribes and Pharisees, you will never enter the kingdom of heaven" (Matt. 5:20).

"Unless you turn and become like children, you will never enter the kingdom of heaven" (Matt. 18:3).

"If any man would come after me, let him deny himself, and take up his cross and follow me. . . . Whoever loses his life for my sake will find it" (Matt. 16:24-25).

Jesus made it crystal clear that anyone who would follow Him should consider carefully that there is a definite cost of discipleship (Luke 14:27-28). There must be surrender to Him as Lord. He himself took the narrow way and called those who would be His disciples to a moral and ethical life consistent with His own. "Enter by the narrow gate," He commanded. " . . . For the gate is narrow and the way is hard that leads to life, and those who find it are few" (Matt. 7:13-14).

Unless these conditions are met we cannot be saved. But, praise God, His grace is available to make obedience possible! We cannot enter God's kingdom unaided, but the wonder is that He has provided completely for our need. He asks nothing that we cannot do. When the Spirit convicts us we *want* to be different! Instead of continuing to be *self*-centered we begin to desire to be *God*-centered and dependent on Him for salvation and life. As we make the response which is within our power, His Spirit accomplishes what we cannot do: He brings us to new birth and into life in Christ.

Christian Standards

Paul never tired of referring to the grace of God, yet he was unwavering in making the Savior's requirements known. Grace was no excuse for sin (Rom. 6:1-4). "Do you not know," he warns, "that the unrighteous will not inherit the kingdom of God? Do not be deceived; neither the immoral, nor idolators, nor adulterers, nor homosexuals, nor thieves, nor the greedy, nor drunkards, nor revilers, nor robbers will inherit the kingdom of God. And such *were* some of you. . ."! (1 Cor. 6:9-11). There was salvation for those who had done these things in the past, but there was no hope if these sins continued as a way of life.

Paul warns others: "Be sure of this, that no immoral or impure man, or one who is covetous . . . has any inheritance in the kingdom of Christ and of God" (Eph. 5:5; see 2 Tim. 2:19).

John similarly comes straight to the point: "If we say we have fellowship with him while we walk in darkness, we lie. . . " (1 John 1:6). Again: "If any one loves the world, love for the Father is not in him" (1 John 2:15). Again: "Beloved, do not imitate evil but imitate good. He who does good is of God; he who does evil has not seen God" (3 John 11).

Peter wrote: "As he who called you is holy, be holy yourselves in all your conduct; since it is written, 'You shall be holy, for I am holy' " (1 Pet. 1:15-16). We are called *away* from sin and sinning, and we are called *to* righteousness and Christlikeness. If we imagine Jesus can be satisfied with any mere outward change of conversation, His own words demonstrate this is a false hope. Not everyone who uses the right and appropriate devotional language shall enter the kingdom, but only he who *does* the will of the Father. Even if some have a prophetic, deliverance and miracle-working ministry, this does not necessarily earn the Lord's approval (1 Cor. 13:2-3). If the inner quality of relationship is lacking, they will hear the Lord's words: "I never knew you; depart from me, you evildoers" (Matt. 7:21-23). It is not sufficient to be a devoted listener to the Lord, for, in a memorable parable Jesus stressed that it was the house of the *obedient* man that was built upon rock and stood firm under test, while the house of the man who heard the Master's words but did not translate them into action, fell (Matt. 7:24-27).

Jesus came not just to change our destiny, but to change our whole pattern of living. He came to lift us out of the environment of sin and transfer us into that of a holy Savior and Lord, where we are controlled by the love of Christ (2 Cor. 5:14). We have been summoned out of darkness to live in light—His light (1 Pet. 2:9; 1 Thess. 4:7; 2 Cor. 7:1; 6:14-18).

The Spirit whom we receive is the *Holy* Spirit. In two out of seven passages describing baptism in the Spirit the experience is described as "being baptized with the Holy Spirit *and with fire*" (Matt. 3:11; Luke 3:16), which points to the Spirit's work of purifying and cleansing the mind and spirit of the believer. Much will still need attention in the daily living of the Spirit-baptized believer but the work has begun and should become increasingly discernable.

"Go, and do not sin again"

One purpose of Jesus' coming is stated early in the gospel. It was said of Mary's holy Baby: "You shall call his name Jesus, for he will save his people from their sins" (Matt. 1:21)—not just from the *guilt* of sin, but *also from the compulsion to sin.* Paul elaborates: "For our sake he made him to be sin who knew no sin, so that in him we might become the righteousness of God" (2 Cor. 5:21). The blood of Jesus cleanses us from all sin (1 John 1:7), but once forgiven, we cannot *presume* on grace. Salvation is free but it is not cheap. When Jesus said to a repentant woman, "Neither do I condemn you," He immediately followed it with, "Go, and do not sin again" (John 8:11).

So, however we try, we cannot side-step the issue: without holiness we cannot see the Lord. Only the pure in heart shall see Him (Heb. 12:14; Matt. 5:8). They alone can enjoy His fellowship. And when we pray, the hands we lift to the Lord must be holy (1 Tim. 2:8), for true worship can come only from clean hands and sanctified hearts. These speak louder than any of our words, for it is *life* that proves reality.

God can sovereignly use an unbeliever like Cyrus to perform His will (Isa. 44:28-45:1; 2 Chron. 36:22-23), or bring a genuine grace-gift through a donkey (Num. 22:23-30)—or inspire someone to speak in tongues, prophesy, exercise a great gift of faith and have knowledge. All of these can be God-given but the channel can still be "nothing" (1 Cor. 13). So even if we are being used by God in these ways, it is hardly the ultimate test of spirituality! God can use a person in spite of himself.

Positive Qualities

The believer is called to demonstrate both the inner and outer characteristics of his Lord; to be increasingly "conformed to the image of God's Son" (Rom. 8:29). As he depends upon the Lord, the Spirit is able to produce a harvest of love, joy, peace, patience, kindness, goodness, faithfulness, gentleness and self-control (Gal.

5:22-23; see the commentary on 1 Cor. 13 in the author's book, *Love and Gifts*).

This is completely opposite to the humanistic observance of a series of do's and don't's. Neither does it result from any self-effected, religious self-improvement program! *This fruit is Spirit-produced*—and, unlike the human product, it will remain when the pressure is on.

Holiness and the fruit of the Spirit can grow and mature only in the environment of relationship—relationship to our Lord Jesus Christ. We follow *Him*! (see John 10:27). *He* is our example, companion, indwelling friend! (1 Pet. 2:21; Matt. 28:20; John 15:4-5, 14-15). We are related to Him, for He is our brother (Matt. 12:50; 28:10; Heb. 2:11-12). We are invited into an intimate relationship of listening, responding to, and following Him. Privilege indeed!

Through this relationship we gain our moral strength and motivation. If Christ abides in us and we in Him, His divine energy enables us to produce worthwhile and lasting fruit (John 15:5)—a harvest of righteousness and Christlikeness. We do not need to struggle and strain to bring forth such fruit, for it cannot be produced by our own self-effort. A tree does not struggle, fret or agonize to bring forth an apple. The fruit forms as a natural result of being united with the life-flow of the tree. It grows out of the relationship it has with the tree. It comes to maturity by "resting." And for the Christian, relationship and rest comes through faith and by continually yielding in obedience to each prompting of the Spirit so that God can have His way. These factors provide the environment for the development and maturing of fruit that brings enjoyment to the Lord.

Practical Instructions

Paul writes to the believers at Colossae: "If then you have been raised with Christ, seek the things that are above, where Christ is, seated at the right hand of God. Set your minds on things that are above, not on things that are on earth. For you have died, and your life is hid with Christ in God. When Christ who is our life appears, then you also will appear with him in glory.

"Put to death therefore what is earthly in you. . . . Put them all away. . . . You have put off the old nature with its practices and have put on the new nature, which is being renewed in knowledge after the image of its creator. . . .

"Put on then, as God's chosen ones, holy and beloved, compassion, kindness, lowliness, meekness, and patience, forbearing one another and, if one has a complaint against another, forgiving each other; as the Lord has forgiven you, so you also must forgive. And above all these put on love. . . . And let the peace of Christ rule in your hearts. . . . And be thankful. Let the word of Christ dwell in you richly, as you teach and admonish one another in all wisdom, and as you sing psalms and hymns and spiritual songs with thankfulness in your hearts to God. And whatever you do, in word or deed, do everything in the name of the Lord Jesus, giving thanks to God the Father through him.

"Wives, be subject. . . . Husbands, love. . . . Children, obey. . . . Fathers, do not provoke. . . . Slaves obey. . . . Whatever your task, work heartily, as serving the Lord and not men, knowing that from the Lord you will receive the inheritance as your reward; you are serving the Lord Christ" (Col. 3; see also Col. 4).

Baptism Pictures Washing and Newness

The baptism that follows commitment to Christ is rich in instruction. It remains like a photograph indelibly printed on the photographic plate of the believer's memory. It is a living picture of cleansing, new life, holiness. By its meaningful and vivid symbolism it impresses upon our mind for all time that the baptismal pool was a "bath" for total cleansing from the moral *stain* of sin. After reminding the Christians of their past, Paul says: "And such were some of you. *But you were washed . . .* " (1 Cor. 6:11; see Matt. 3:6; Acts 2:38; 22:16). So baptism becomes a silent admission that we needed cleansing, and have found it through trusting Christ and through responding to His command to be baptized. Therefore, it also *becomes a determined and public committal to a new manner and a new standard of life.* We have been *washed*—to live a clean life.

Another aspect of baptism that especially relates to holiness is that union with Christ, crucified and risen, is the only way to newness of life. Immersion in the baptismal pool symbolizes life coming only through death. It points to the death, burial and resurrection, not only of our Lord, but of the candidate himself. So when we are baptized we stand forward and confess ourselves dead to our old ways. We desire to be buried. We say in effect: "I have died; bury me." Our old life is then put out of sight as it is buried in the watery grave. Then, from the old, emergence from the waters signifies newness of life in Christ. The new and risen life is entered upon only through the death and burial of the man that was (Rom. 6). From now on we live on the cleansed and resurrection side of the pool.

True Holiness Attracts

Holiness is not a cold and forbidding thing. It cannot be separated from love—and love attracts, warms. Even though a sight of the Lord brought devastating self-realization to Isaiah, it also won his heart, and made him volunteer to be the Lord's willing servant. "Here I am! Send me," he said (Isa. 6:8). Though the death of a perfect Savior passed judgment on all sin, the magnetism of the Cross was real. It melted and drew rebellious, proud and self-sufficient hearts. It gave new hope to the outcast and sinner, and kindled a desire to share the same love and mercy that they had found.

There was an attractiveness that rested upon the early Christians. There was a beauty in their holiness, and they soon found favor wherever there were sincere people (Acts 2:47). Hypocrisy and unreality were scorched by the blazing purity of God's holy fire, yet the fire also warmed, and people were attracted and won. Through brokenness and death to self, love was released. It was not remote or coldly correct. The characteristics of love found in 1 Corinthians 13 were becoming obvious to the believers' pagan friends who could readily see that these Christians were Christ's disciples, who genuinely loved one another (John 13:35). It was this holy love of Jesus that drew and conquered Paul (Gal. 2:20), and made him delight to call himself a slave of Jesus Christ.

Becoming More Like the Lord

God's purpose for us is stated repeatedly, but nowhere more clearly than in 2 Cor. 3:17-18: "Now the Lord is the Spirit, and where the Spirit of the Lord is, there is freedom. And we all, with unveiled face, beholding the glory of the Lord, are being changed into his likeness from one degree of glory to another; for this comes from the Lord who is the Spirit."

Under the old dispensation, only one man, Moses, gazed with unveiled face upon the glory of the Lord (2 Cor. 3:7-13). But now in the new age, the dispensation of the Spirit, *every* child of God has the privilege of gazing on His glory. The veil of sin and unbelief which shut off the vista of such splendor has been removed through the blood of the cross and faith in Christ.

We are called to the unspeakable privilege of beholding the Lord and speaking with Him. And as we do so, we become changed into His likeness in ever-increasing measure. His character, actions and reactions in all their strength and tenderness become the inspiration of our own. We become more and more like Him. As we behold Him He progressively transforms us. (The word translated "changed" [*metamorphoō*] is the same as that used when Jesus was "transfigured" on the mountain.)

It is quite impossible for us to set ourselves free from sin or change ourselves into His likeness. While we must cooperate with the Lord, it is ultimately only by the operation of the sanctifying Spirit of Jesus that we are changed. And finally, when Jesus appears, the growing resemblance to Him becomes complete, for then we shall be like Him (1 John 3:2).

Meanwhile, our task is to follow His example. He could say: "I do nothing on my own authority but *speak thus as the Father taught me.* . . . I always do what is pleasing to *him.* . . . *I do as the Father has commanded me*" (John 8:28-29; 14:31).

We, too, need to speak as the Father teaches us and do what is pleasing to Him. But because we are very human we will often need to get on our knees and humbly give back to the Lord the spiritual gifts He has been manifesting through us, so that He can purify them and enable us to bring the Lord's message with the same spirit that He himself would manifest. Only as He deals with our human spirit are we able increasingly to speak as oracles of God (1 Pet. 4:10-11).

Jesus had no self-will, and was sensitive to every communication from His Father. His body, character and openness to the Father's voice provided a perfect vehicle for the Spirit's unhindered activity. He did not need to strive, shout or harangue. He did not judge by outward appearances. Meekness and gentleness were His method. Righteousness and truth were His belt (Isa. 42:1-4; 11:1-5; 61:1-3; 40:11). He was completely pure and had nothing within His life to give Satan access. Satan therefore had no power over Him or His spirit (John 14:30).

So with us, the more developed becomes our relationship with the Lord the greater degree of Christlikeness is attained. Satan is then starved out, our freedom and authority increase, and we become less liable to deception.

Relationship to Christ by the power of the Spirit is the key factor, and the fruit of the Spirit, holiness and our service grows naturally out of that relationship.

Jesus prayed: "This is eternal life, that they *know* thee the only true God, and Jesus Christ whom thou hast sent" (John 17:3). Paul affirmed: "I count everything as loss because of the surpassing worth of *knowing* Christ Jesus my Lord. For his sake I have suffered the loss of all things, and count them as refuse, *in order that*

I may gain Christ and be found in him, not having a righteousness of my own, based on law, but that which is through faith in Christ, the righteousness from God that depends on faith; *that I may know him* and the power of his resurrection . . . " (Phil. 3:8-10).

This makes holiness positive rather than negative, attractive rather than repelling.

5

Events at Pentecost

Not long before Jesus was crucified He said to His disciples, "It is to your advantage that I go away, for if I do not go away the Counselor will not come to you; but if I go, I will send him to you . . . and he will glorify me . . . " (John 16:7, 14).

Until Jesus had completed His redemptive task at Calvary and risen again the Spirit could not be sent: until then, the benefits of the New Covenant could not be given.

After the crucifixion with all its apparent tragedy there came the triumphant day of resurrection when the Lord Jesus presented himself alive to His rejoicing disciples. Then He breathed on them and said, "Receive the Holy Spirit." And at that moment a new depth of relationship was established between Jesus and His followers, and a greater authority was given them (John 20:21-23).

Yet there was more to follow. The full outward expression and release of the Spirit had to wait until the post-resurrection appearances were over. First Jesus had come to breathe His Spirit of life into the disciples, but soon He would come afresh with a greater purpose and in fullness (Acts 1:5).[1]

The Day of Pentecost

After Ascension Day the disciples spent ten long days without contact with Jesus while they waited for "the promise of the Father" to be fulfilled, although what that might mean was still very much a mystery to them. They did know, however, that they were missing contact with their Lord and were yearning for fellowship to be somehow restored. Meanwhile with one mind they sought Him as they continued steadfastly in prayer (Acts 1:14-15).

"And suddenly a sound came from heaven like the rush of a mighty wind, and it filled all the house where they were sitting. And there appeared to them tongues as of fire, distributed and resting on each one of them. And they were all filled with the Holy Spirit and began to speak in other tongues, as the Spirit gave them utterance" (Acts 2:1-4).

The Spirit, who is also called the Spirit of Jesus (Acts 16:7; Phil. 1:19), came to flood and fill them with himself. As a result, their Savior and Master suddenly became wonderfully real to each one of them. By the Spirit their Lord was there! He was real! He was back with them, to remain with them always.

All this immediately brought them into an entirely new and spiritual dimension of knowledge through the Spirit, and it immediately became natural to be occupied with the Lord and to praise and worship Him for His mighty acts of salvation.

The time would soon come to minister to others, but the need of the moment was to magnify the Lord Jesus in their own hearts first. They would bring the firstfruits to Him. First they would break their alabaster box and pour out the fragrant offering of their individual and corporate praise and adoration in languages given by the Spirit, though the words themselves were foreign to their own ears. Certainly their own words were inadequate; too limited to declare their great Redeemer's praise. Out of abundance their mouths would speak, for God had filled their hearts, and they must first commune with Him (Matt. 12:34; 1 Cor. 14:2).

But the languages could not be concealed, and they quickly attracted the attention of the Jews and proselytes who overheard the enthusiastic Christians. These outsiders now came together, drawn by curiosity and the dynamism within the group. And as they listened they realized they were eavesdropping (see also Acts 16:25), as they heard "the mighty works of God" being extolled in the language of their birth (Acts 2:11). Praise and glory were being offered to the Lord. Yet others who were drawn by the worship reacted negatively in unbelief and ridicule (Acts 2:13). It is clear that those who desired to understand the praise being offered could do so, but the Lord would not reveal himself in blessing to those who would despise His outpouring.

Similarities and Differences

On the Day of Pentecost the tongues were *foreign languages unknown to the speakers* but recognized by the hearers, whereas Paul and the Corinthians spoke in *unrecognized languages*. This latter variety also occurred in Samaria, Caesarea and Ephesus (Acts 8, 10, 19), for there is no mention of recognizable tongues there.

The Lord in His sovereignty gives *various* kinds of tongues (1 Cor. 12:10). These can be human or heavenly languages (1 Cor. 13:1). At Pentecost the listeners heard a unique form of tongues in recognized foreign languages, but whether recognizable or unrecognized, in all cases they had this in common: *the languages were entirely unknown to the speakers*, and were never the product of their own mind.

Even at Pentecost tongues were not directed to men but to God, for (a) there is no suggestion that they were speaking in tongues to others (Acts 2:4); (b) they were speaking in tongues among themselves before the multitude came together (Acts 2:6), and even if the crowd had never gathered, they would have continued to offer the firstfruits of their Spirit-inspired adoration to Him; and (c) the tongues were not necessary for communication with the multitude because Peter spoke to them all afterwards, not in tongues but in normal speech, and without the need of translation or interpretation (Acts 2:14). That the 120 were indeed praying, and primarily speaking to God, is confirmed by Paul's explicit teaching on the purpose of tongues (1 Cor. 14:2, 14).

Special Purpose of Tongues

What then was the *special* purpose in having foreign tongues on this occasion? What was the purpose in addressing *the Lord* in say, the Cappadocian dialect?

The difference on the Day of Pentecost was not in the essential nature of tongues as prayer, for it remained communication with God wherever it was exercised.

Here at Pentecost the Father would receive spiritual worship from His children, but in addition He would use tongues and the testimony of Peter linked with it to vindicate Jesus as Messiah, and to acknowledge those who were His people. But He had yet a further purpose. At this, the commencement of Christian ministry in the power of the Spirit, He would use tongues as an encouraging, confirming sign to Christians that they would be given power to witness to all the nations of the world as Jesus had said. And so at Pentecost, besides the adoration offered to the Lord there was a double sign: a clear sign to both Christians and non-Christians of God's vindication of Jesus as Lord, and a sign to God's people of His love for the whole world. It advertised His intention to be known far beyond the limited area of Palestine, and demonstrated His ability to empower His Church for its worldwide task. So in Acts 2, besides its basic purpose of prayer we have an extended use of tongues by the Spirit. In God's sovereignty, this miracle has occurred on occasions since Pentecost. Nevertheless, it is a divine extention of the usual purpose of speaking in tongues.

6

Are Gifts Intended for Us Today?

"Love never ends; as for prophecy, it will pass away; as for tongues, they will cease; as for knowledge, it will pass away. For our knowledge is imperfect and our prophecy is imperfect; but when the perfect comes, the imperfect will pass away. When I was a child, I spoke like a child, I thought like a child, I reasoned like a child; when I became a man, I gave up childish ways. For now we see in a mirror dimly, but then face to face. Now I know in part; then I shall understand fully, even as I have been fully understood" (1 Cor. 13:8-12).

It has sometimes been argued that God gave revelation and other gifts until the death of the last apostle, by which time the full Scriptures had been written and there was no longer need for further revelation. With the completion of Scripture the perfect is said to have come and revelation therefore passed away!

This view must be rejected on various grounds.

Biblical and Historical Evidence

It is too restrictive to confine the purpose of revelation solely to the writing of Scripture, for it was also given to enhance, complement, amplify, illustrate or personally apply God's truths and to convict or strengthen people. When this was its purpose revelation could parallel recorded truth but it would never contradict it. We know that there were many Spirit-inspired events and revelations during the original apostles' lifetime that are omitted from the biblical record, for these had a personal, local or passing application (2 Cor. 12:1-4, 12; Acts 5:12; 6:8-10; 14:3-4; 21:9; Rom. 15:17-19; 1 Pet. 4:10).

The literature of the post-apostolic age also contradicts the view that the gifts were in fact withdrawn, for there is ample historic evidence that the gifts continued into the second and third centuries.

Irenaeus, for example, lived between A.D. 130-200, and he testified that gifts were continuing among Christians. He wrote: "For some do certainly and truly drive out demons,[1] so that those who have thus been cleansed from evil spirits frequently both believe and join themselves to the Church. Others have foreknowledge of things to come: they see visions, and utter prophetic expressions. Others still, heal the sick by laying their hands upon them and they are made whole. Yea, moreover, as I have said, the dead even have been raised up and remained among us for many years.

"*And what shall I more say? It is not possible to name the number of gifts* which the Church, throughout the whole world, has received from God, in the name of Jesus Christ, who was crucified under Pontius Pilate *and which she exerts day by day* for the benefit of the Gentiles, neither practising deception upon any, nor taking any reward from them. For as she has received freely from God, freely also does she minister."

Later, he wrote: "For this reason does the apostle declare, 'We speak wisdom among them that are perfect' (1 Cor. 2:6), terming those persons 'perfect' who have received the Spirit of God, and who through the Spirit of God do speak in all languages, as he used himself also to speak. In like manner we do also hear many brethren in the Church, who possess prophetic gifts, and who through the Spirit speak all kinds of languages, and bring to light for the general benefit the hidden things of man, and declare the mysteries of God."[2]

Tertullian (c. A.D. 160-222) also referred to continuing manifestations. He first challenged the gnostic Marcion to exhibit as gifts of his god people who could prophesy, lay open the secrets of the heart, produce a psalm, vision, prayer, or interpretation of tongues by the inspiration of the Holy Spirit. Tertullian then continued: "*Now all these signs [of spiritual gifts] are forthcoming from my side without any difficulty. . . .* Here, then, is my frank avowal for any one who cares to require it."[3]

A prophecy through Melito of Sardis is recorded later in chapter fourteen of this book and bears the same graphic testimony to the continuance of spiritual gifts among the people of God. It is dated somewhere between A.D. 170-195.

Apparently revelation ceased to function only when the Church became institutionalized and had declined spiritually. John Wesley once wrote that he was fully convinced that "the grand reason why the miraculous gifts were so soon withdrawn, was not only

faith and holiness were well nigh lost, but that dry, formal, orthodox men began even then to ridicule whatever gifts they had
not themselves; and to decry them all as either madness or im-
posture."

Perfection Comes When Jesus Comes

When Paul speaks about "the perfect" coming, he can be
referring only to the time when Jesus returns and brings us into
God's immediate presence. When Jesus comes, perfection comes.
We shall then be perfect like He is (1 John 3:2).

Donald Bridge and David Phypers have written: "Clearly Paul
is looking forward to a time yet future when not only colourful
spiritual gifts but virtually everything that makes up normal life
will have passed away in the final glorious fulfilment of the promises of God."[4] When Paul wrote to the Corinthians, saying, "You
are not lacking in any spiritual gift, as you wait for the revealing
of our Lord Jesus Christ" (1 Cor. 1:7), he showed he had no
place in his theology for these gifts ceasing before Christ's return.

Paul's argument in 1 Cor. 13:8-12 can be summarized as follows:
The gifts will pass away because they are imperfect in their operation. They will pass away when the perfect comes. They shall
neither pass away until that time nor continue beyond that time.
When the perfect comes we shall no longer see imperfectly but
face to face: we shall no longer have imperfect knowledge but
perfect knowledge and perfect sight.

No Change in the Gifts

Others agree that "the perfect" refers to the time when
we see the Lord "face to face," yet they claim the *original*
gifts have undergone a fundamental change over the years—a
metamorphosis. They believe prophecy has changed into preaching or teaching, tongues into poetry or Bible translation, and God-
imparted words of knowledge into theology. This too is a theory
drawn out of midair, and without a syllable of biblical authority
to back it.

Theological considerations as well as textual ones confirm that
all the New Testament gifts are meant for us today. In apostolic
times the Church was active in attacking the powers of darkness.
Paul could say: "Though we live in the world, we are not carrying
on a worldly war, for the weapons of our warfare are not worldly,
but have divine power to destroy strongholds" (2 Cor. 10:3-4).

We live in the same world and in the same dispensation as the apostles did, engaged in the same war, with the strongholds of evil still in fierce conflict with God's way and God's people. If gifts were needed then they are needed now!

Satan has not suspended his activities just because the canon has been completed, or because the original apostles established the Church in strategic but limited regions. He is not as silly as that! Until the spiritual war is won at the coming of Christ, we need the same spiritual weapons to fight the same attacks of the enemy of human souls and bodies. Seen differently, these weapons are not only weapons of warfare, but also weapons of Christ's love, used by Him to release captives whom Satan has bound, and to set the oppressed at liberty. Because of the spiritual nature of all the gifts there is universal need for their benefits today and until Jesus returns.

Until that day, all expressions of the Spirit's life are as necessary for the Church as physical members are to the human body (see 1 Cor. 12:14-26). The early Christians did not liken the Spirit's gifts to some unimportant, secondary, infantile or transitory function. They considered them as indispensable and permanent as are the functions of feet, hands, ears, eyes and nose to the life and health of the body. The body never outgrows these organs. If they were removed the body would either die or remain as a sad testimony to its sickness and impotence.

It is nowhere even hinted that immediately upon the death of the last original apostle Christians would be so transformed that these gifts would become redundant. Until our Lord returns triumphant, these gifts are no more open to cancellation than are His promises. We cannot logically reject them when it is self-evident that no Christian is yet fully edified. Certainly, to be consistent, we cannot retain love because it edifies yet reject any gift which also edifies (1 Cor. 8:1; 14:2-5, 26-31).

In an earlier chapter we saw the essential relationship between the fullness and the gifts of the Spirit. Because of this connection, any denial that the gifts are for today becomes a denial that the fullness of the Spirit is for today. That too must be sacrificed.

Donald Bridge and David Phypers have noted how the gift-withdrawal theory poses a problem to those who wish to use the New Testament as their handbook for the Church today, for they give examples of how the "ordinary" is mixed inextricably with the supernatural. They comment: "The two strands cannot be separated without destroying the whole. If one strand is not applicable today, the account ceases to be a guide in our situation and becomes only of historical interest. And we have nothing with which to replace it. . . . The Epistles . . . are concerned primarily with sound doctrine and holy living—as all Christians should be. But when they do touch on the subject of the exercise of the gifts, they tell their readers how to regulate them, how to test them, how to recognize them, how to exercise them—never how to phase them out. . . . The only actual biblical instruction available on the subject assumes the presence of the gifts." [5]

Exactly!

7

Should Every Christian Be Able to Speak in Tongues and Prophesy?

Speaking in Tongues

Should all speak in tongues? The answer is simply, "No" in one context and "Yes" in another. Only some will be inspired in any particular worship service to bring an authoritative utterance in tongues, in which case the additional gift of interpretation is necessary. On the other hand, in private, and for an individual's prayer and praise during public worship, all may speak in tongues.

Scripture clearly establishes that *speaking in tongues is for every Christian for personal communion with the Lord.*

1. *It is the plain meaning of the phrase, "I want you all to speak in tongues" (1 Cor. 14:5).* Paul could say elsewhere, "I appeal to you therefore, brethren, . . . to present your bodies as a living sacrifice, holy and acceptable to God" (Rom. 12:1), and we know he expressed God's will for all. He showed equally clearly that all are meant to be filled with the Spirit (Eph. 5:18). Scripture teaches that *all* have sinned, *all* can come to Jesus in their weariness, and *all* Christians can partake of the bread and the cup (Rom. 3:23; Matt. 11:28; 26:27). Paul is equally emphatic about tongues. No one need make the mistake of thinking this practice may *not* be for him: he wants *all* to speak in tongues.[1] [2] It too is a gift everyone can exercise. While God gives His gifts "as he wills," that will is openly declared on tongues just as it is on salvation in Christ. In similar fashion, the Son gives life "to whom he will" (John 5:21), but whoever will may come and find himself included (see Rev. 22:17).

When Paul wrote: "I want you all to speak in tongues," his words were directed to Christians everywhere (1 Cor. 1:2). Yet they did not represent his own personal whim: behind them was the Holy Spirit, the true author. The Spirit would not inspire the apostle to say he wanted all Christians to exercise this gift, and then make it available for only a few of them.

2. *Paul can envisage the whole congregation speaking in tongues.* If it were not possible for all the Christians present to speak in tongues in their assembly, Paul's comment in 1 Cor. 14:23 becomes quite meaningless and absurd. It was, however, just as possible for all the Christians to speak in tongues as it was for outsiders or unbelievers to enter their meeting. Paul was not, of course, commending them for speaking in tongues without wisdom or consideration for others, but there is no thought that they were engaging in counterfeit or merely human activity.

3. *The harmony of scripture supports this understanding.* On a first reading of 1 Cor. 12:30 and 14:5 modern readers might think that Paul was contradicting himself. But, to say nothing of his writing under the inspiration of the Spirit, Paul as an intelligent man would have hardly committed such a foolish mistake as to contradict himself within the short space of 19 verses.

The statements are clearly harmonized by the simple fact that while it was God's will that everyone should speak in tongues in personal communion with the Lord, only a few in a meeting were anointed to bring a public utterance. This distinction in Paul's mind between tongues as a means of public ministry, and their personal, individual use would be instantly apparent to his readers.

The only alternative to this explanation is that Paul did not know his own mind, and that his will was not God's will on this matter. But such an idea cannot stand, for Paul did not write simply as a private person. He was God's inspired mouthpiece (1 Cor. 14:37-39; 2 Tim. 3:16).

4. *All have equal opportunity to pray with their spirit.* Every Christian needs to speak to God. Since speaking to God in tongues is another important aspect of the prayer life which even a mature apostle continued to value highly (1 Cor. 14:2, 14-15, 18), the case is strong for its availability to believers with less maturity and who therefore have greater need of strengthening. Paul communed with God in tongues as well as with his understanding, and by emphasizing this fact he implied that his readers should do the same.

God is impartial (Rom. 2:11; Gal. 2:6; Eph. 6:9) and He has given to every Christian a human spirit and an equal opportunity to pray on that same level of the spirit (1 Cor. 14:14-16, 5). *Each* Christian is to use "*every kind* of prayer and entreaty" (Eph. 6:18, various versions), for the total range of prayer is available to all God's people.

After Pentecost, tongues would be included with other forms of prayer under the general terms of prayer and praise (see Acts 2:42-47).

5. *Spirit-inspired praise is required from every Christian.* Praise and thanksgiving similarly are a necessary discipline and privilege for every believer to bring to the Lord (Ps. 50:14-15, 23; 22:3; 1 Pet. 2:9; Eph. 1:3-14; Phil. 1:9-11). And since the gift of tongues is an important means of Spirit-inspired praise (1 Cor. 14:16-17; Acts 2:11; 10:46) that is not made superfluous by praise in natural speech—for it supplies a need not met in any other way—this is a further indication that God has made it available for everyone. Paul praised God with his new tongue as well as in his natural speech. (Spirit-inspired praise is considered again on a related subject in point four of the next chapter.)

6. *Every God-given means of upbuilding is available for every Christian.* Not every *responsibility* or *office* in the church is intended for everyone. But throughout the New Testament it is made clear that there are many "means of grace," that is, means given by God's grace for seeking and receiving grace. All these are available and intended for every Christian. There are no exceptions.

Every Christian needs upbuilding. By tracing the biblical usage of the word *oikodomeō* (to build up, edify), we see that every Christian can enjoy edifying life in Christ and God and His Word (Col. 2:7; Acts 20:32); and everyone is instructed to build himself up on his most holy faith and to pray in the Holy Spirit (Jude 20). Jesus, the Holy Spirit, baptism, the Lord's Supper, the Word of God, love, prayer and praise all edify the believer, and as such, are for every Christian. There were no specially privileged "gnostic" Christians, for *all* had access to the same mysteries: *every* man was being taught in *all* wisdom (Col. 1:28; see 1 Cor. 14:2). Citing Col. 1:28, F. F. Bruce writes: "There is no part of Christian teaching that is to be reserved for a spiritual elite. All the truth of God is for all the people of God. . . . There are no heights in Christian attainment which are not within the reach of all, by the power of divine grace."[3]

Since tongues are a most valuable aid to spiritual growth and balance (1 Cor. 14:4), and one which, like other forms of prayer, can be exercised by the individual believer in his communion with God, it would be a contradiction of the Father's nature (Matt. 7:11; 6:9-11) if He gave this provision to some of His children yet withheld it from others.

7. *Sincerity demands it.* It would be obnoxious for Paul to say, "I thank God I speak in tongues more than you all . . . and I want you all to speak in tongues," if he knew that most could never experience the same sense of rejoicing that he obviously had, or if the same strengthening exercise was completely denied them (1 Cor. 14:18, 4). It would be deceitful to praise before the church and commend to all his Christian readers something that would be completely contrary to God's will for some of them. Certainly it would shock them after the inspiration of the gracious and thoughtful attitudes of the preceding "love" chapter.

Paul did not tell half-truths, or speak with tongue in cheek. Yes meant Yes, and No meant No (2 Cor. 1:17-18). It would be completely out of character for him to vacillate on a matter such as this. We cannot imagine him saying, for example: "Now I want you *all* to speak in tongues—but even as I write this I am certain that few of you will ever be able to do so. Tongues are spiritually constructive, and therefore beneficial to your life in God—yet I am convinced that God gives most of you no chance whatever of profiting from this means of spiritual growth and sensitivity to the Lord. Speaking in tongues is prayer with the spirit, by the Holy Spirit's enabling, which I for my part am determined to continue exercising (1 Cor. 14:15)—but I know that most of you are never meant to experience it for yourselves. The gift of tongues is also acceptable praise and thanksgiving in the area of the spirit—but God has made that possible for only a very limited few. Be imitators of me (1 Cor. 4:16; 11:1; Phil. 3:17; 1 Thess. 1:6)—but in a major area of prayer, praise and spiritual growth you are denied what I experience."

A double-minded man is unstable in all his ways (James 1:7-8), yet Paul would be such a man if he knew his expressed desire that all his readers speak in tongues was unable to be realized. To hold up before the vast majority that which you know to be completely unattainable and praise its merits is not only insensitive, but irresponsible and sub-Christian, and in stark contrast with Paul's whole spirit and words in 1 Corinthians 13. Conversely, if the gift can in fact be desired and acquired with Paul's blessing, his words stimulate and encourage, for all can enjoy the same means of edifying.

8. *Historical evidence supports it.* That tongues are a gift for all Christians is further supported by the historical evidence in Acts. This shows that in each case where speaking in tongues is recorded, the gift was received, not just by a select few, not even by the majority, but by the total number of Christians present. *Did* all speak in tongues? At Jerusalem the answer was, "Yes, all 120 disciples who were present," for "they were all filled . . . and began to speak in other tongues" (Acts 1:15; 2:4). Again, at Caesarea, many people had gathered and they all spoke in tongues, for "the Holy Spirit fell on all who heard the word . . . for they heard them speaking in tongues and extolling God" (Acts 10:27, 44-46). Then, too, the total group of about twelve in Ephesus all spoke in tongues, for "the Holy Spirit came on them; and they spoke with tongues and prophesied" (Acts 19:6-7).

Certainly in these three cases where tongues are specifically mentioned there were not "only two, or at most three, and each in turn," with one to interpret (1 Cor. 14:27). Instead they all spoke in tongues, all together, and with no interpretation—and they were obviously in the will of God.

How then do we piece together these two strands?

If the Christians we meet within Acts had been asked: "Do you all bring *to your public worship* an authoritative word in tongues?", their answer would have been: "No. Definitely not! We can all pray in tongues privately, and of course we should be doing this consistently, and in the congregation as well, in quiet communion with God. Yet only a very limited number will receive an anointing (a special direction and enabling) in a meeting to bring a public utterance in tongues, and in that case interpretation is required. On any occasion two or three of our number may bring a gift of tongues and present it before the assembly. At another time perhaps two different ones will be anointed to bring tongues, while others will receive the interpretation. Speaking in tongues is complete in itself between a man and his God, but where God gives to one of us a special anointing to bring an authoritative utterance in tongues, His purpose is different: He now desires to build up the church, and to this end the twin gift of interpretation is required so that we all can be built up by the inspired word which has been given."

So, to refrain from speaking in tongues in private or public is to refrain from taking advantage of a God-given provision and aid to spiritual growth.

An Objection Considered

Some have nevertheless concluded that tongues cannot be meant for all Christians because although the 120 and some others are specifically said to speak in tongues, the book of Acts is silent in regard to tongues-speaking by the 3000 (Acts 2:32-41), the Ethiopian (8:34-39), Lydia and her household (16:13-15), the Philippian jailer (16:25-34), those at Athens (17:32-34), and others.

But in spite of these examples the objection is invalid, for frequently the obvious and conventional pattern is assumed without description. For example: 1. Acts records only Jerusalem and Troas over a 30-year period as centers where the Lord's Supper was observed (daily in Jerusalem at first, and once at Troas, Acts 2:41-42; 20:7-11). A doctrine built upon Luke's silence over the various places and occasions where the Supper took place would result in widespread error.

2. In the majority of cases in Acts (20 out of 29) where we could expect baptism to follow heart response it is unrecorded.[4] Yet it would be plainly irresponsible to assume that in 70 percent of cases the Church overlooked baptism, simply because Luke generally failed to mention it.

3. In the 29 cases of response to the Christian message in Acts there is not a single reference to *repentance* actually occurring. Did it not then occur? Surely Luke expected his readers to assume it, not just for the original congregation where it was first commanded, but throughout his whole book, in the light of the words spoken to the audience in Acts 2:38 and 3:19.

4. Though Luke knew that speaking in tongues and other gifts occurred in Corinth, it was totally superfluous for him to relate such widely known information. Likewise, he never once mentioned that Paul prayed in tongues, not because Paul did not do so, but because it was already common knowledge.[5]

So when Luke conserves his valuable space to record the most important developments in the Church's history, it would be foolish to construe his silence on Church order, baptism, gifts and the observance of the Supper to mean that in certain places they were absent. Similarly, his failure to mention tongues at Corinth and in the personal life of Paul at Ephesus, even though it was common knowledge that Paul and the Corinthians exercised this gift, demonstrates that any argument that prayer in tongues only occurred if Luke actually recorded it would be an elementary error in common sense. It flies in the face of known facts. Equally, Luke did not repeat throughout Acts that later believers also fellowshipped together, followed the apostles' teaching, partook of the Supper, and prayed and praised God (Acts 2:42, 46-47). Once these were fully established they did not need to be restated.

It is more relevant to our present purpose to note that wherever the reception or gift of the Holy Spirit is actually described speaking in tongues is conjoined with the reception. Conversely, where tongues are not mentioned in various places, neither is there any reference whatever to the Holy Spirit being received. In only four of 29 cases of heart response is it said that the Spirit was actually received, but in each of these four cases it is mentioned explicitly (Acts 2, 10, 19) or implicitly (Acts 8) that He was received with tongues, though in the latter reference other supernatural manifestations may have been present also. (In Paul's case, the reception is anticipated, but Luke does not pause to acknowledge that it did in fact take place. He assumed the regular pattern without description.) But today it is never assumed that *only* these four groups of Christians received the Spirit, and neither can it be inferred that only these Christians received the gift of tongues.

Anyone who denies that the 3000 (and the others earlier mentioned) spoke in tongues, because it is not recorded, logically has to deny that they repented and received remission of sins and the Spirit, since these are also unrecorded! Thus the Bible teaches in many ways that speaking in tongues is valuable, and that God intended every believer to continue to exercise this gift.

In the next two chapters we will consider whether baptism in the Spirit is always accompanied by speaking to the Lord in tongues. Yet whether we link the commencement of tongues with "baptism in the Spirit," "initial fullness of the Spirit," or any other term, the gift of tongues is shown to be a basic part of the Christian gospel and Christian life, part of God's good news for His people. How ever many experiences of God's grace a Christian may have had, Scripture leaves no doubt that the Father offers this gift to His children and the sooner each begins exercising it the sooner the benefits apply. Paul's divinely given words, "I want you all to speak in tongues," are still true for every Christian.

Prophecy

Can prophecy be manifested by all Christians, or only by a select few?

Paul says less on this point than on tongues, but what he does say demonstrates clearly that all can prophesy.

Moses had earlier yearned: "Would that *all* the Lord's people were prophets, that the Lord would put his Spirit upon them!" (Num. 11:29). Though not all would become *prophets* with a continuing and developed prophetic ministry (1 Cor. 12:29), Paul reveals that every Christian can prophesy under the Spirit's inspiration, and bring edification to the church (1 Cor. 14:31).

The fact that all are to make love their aim, all are earnestly to desire spiritual gifts in general, and all are especially to desire prophecy, underlines that it is open to everyone. Paul's instruction: "Now I want you *all* . . . to prophesy" (1 Cor. 14:5), plus his words: "But if *all* prophesy . . ." (1 Cor. 14:24; see Acts 19:6), shows that he can envisage each of his Christian readers doing so.

While everyone must be receptive to the Lord and earnestly desire this gift, there must first be a revelation and an anointing, for no one can prophesy at will.

And as God requires clean hands and a pure heart for standing in His holy place and receiving revelation by His Spirit (Ps. 24:3-5), we all should be so "standing in his counsel" (Jer. 23:16-22) and walking in holiness, that the Lord can entrust us, as stewards, with this edifying gift for His Body.

In all our seeking of the will of God our aim should never be to try to find reasons for remaining without any aspect of His gracious will and provision. We should not ask: What is the least, but what is the most we can have in the Lord? Some people are clearly anxious to prove to themselves and others that they can dismiss certain spiritual gifts as irrelevant or even harmful to their own personal experience. Yet such a negative and faithless approach to God's Word on *any* aspect of His provision is certain to result in sub-standard Christian living not only for themselves but for the Church as well. It cannot be otherwise, for it represents the very antithesis of faith.

As stated earlier, God distributes His bounty as He wills (1 Cor. 12:11, 18; Heb. 2:4). Yet as clearly as His will is declared on the matter of love, on who can receive the gift of salvation, and on who should present their bodies as a living sacrifice (e.g.,

1 Cor. 13; 2 Pet. 3:9; Rom. 12:1), so it is openly declared on tongues and prophecy (1 Cor. 14:5, 37-38). In some matters and on some gifts God's will may be obscure. For example, Paul does not say: "I thank God I work miracles more than all of you, and I want you all to work miracles—or have gifts of healings." But when he gives direction on tongues and prophecy, he is certain of the will of God and makes that will known. Whatever else is said about the other gifts, this remains certain—tongues and prophecy are intended for every believer.

8

Are Tongues the Initial Sign of Baptism in the Spirit?

Scripture depicts a wide variety of spiritual experiences and a wide variety of spiritual gifts. Yet there is very strong evidence that of this great variety, the particular gift of speaking in tongues became the objective initial sign that the early Christians had received the Holy Spirit. From Pentecost onward, this, apparently, was the particular charismatic gift, the visible and external mark or "seal" which God gave and affixed to mark the reception of the Spirit (2 Cor. 1:22; Eph. 1:13; 4:30; Rom. 8:23).[1]

Three points should be stressed at the outset. First, this study concerns the *initial* sign of receiving the Spirit. We wholeheartedly agree that there are many further evidences of the Spirit's presence and character-transforming power which must subsequently appear in the Christian's life. Second, it is the *scriptural* sign or signs we wish to discover. Our appeal, therefore, cannot be to tradition or to our own or others' experiences, but to the Scriptures, for they present our only reliable and God-given teaching and norm. Third, our concern is not to look into any and every experience which some may call "baptism in the Spirit," for some use the term loosely and wrongly to refer to any spiritual blessing they have had. In our first chapter we showed not only the initiatory but also the overwhelming nature of baptism in the Spirit as found in Scripture, and now we endeavor to discern what particular sign or signs accompanied this experience.

It is realized, of course, that not all will agree with my conclusions, which are stated as firmly as I believe the evidence justifies. The study itself, however, is presented to inform and to encourage a serious examination of the Scriptures. Every Christian can therefore decide before the Lord whether there is biblical evidence for these conclusions, which he can accordingly accept or reject. If you disagree, thinking the evidence is not as strong as I see it to be, at least you will know why many Christians believe as they do. And above all, whether we agree or disagree, we can continue to worship the Lord together and love and respect each other in Christian fellowship. It is in this spirit that this study is presented.

Reasons for Regarding Tongues as the Initial Scriptural Evidence of Baptism in the Spirit

1. Of the four passages which relate that believers were baptized in the Spirit, three state explicitly that tongues occurred, and, in these cases, without exception, everyone baptized in the Spirit spoke in tongues.

(a) At Pentecost 120 people were initially filled with the Spirit and this was marked by speaking in tongues (Acts 1:15; 2:4). Here there was not one but 120 cases of baptism in the Holy Spirit, all of which were accompanied by this manifestation. If the Lord had wanted to establish alternative signs of Holy Spirit baptism, such a large number of people provided Him with an ideal opportunity to establish a great variety of evidence—or some alternatives at least. He could have inspired some to receive with one sign and some with another. Yet not only did some five, forty or ninety percent receive the Spirit with tongues—while the remainder received with various other evidences: instead, as a result of receiving the Spirit, everyone, one hundred percent, spoke in tongues.

On that day there was also a sound "like the rush of a mighty wind" and the appearance of "tongues as of fire." These were awesome signs of the Lord's presence but they were additional to, and clearly not alternative, signs of baptism in the Spirit. We will consider them in more detail later.

(b) At Caesarea where Cornelius and many others were gathered the Christians immediately recognized that the Holy Spirit had fallen on all without exception, "for they heard them speaking in tongues and extolling God" (Acts 10:24-27, 44-47). Proof of the Spirit's outpouring was not that they now trusted Christ, confessed their faith, were baptized, led people to the Lord, had love or a wonderful feeling, glorified Christ in their lives, had grown in holiness or had been prayed for in faith with laying on of hands. The sole evidence was that they spoke in tongues. This was the only expression required to prove the genuineness of Spirit baptism, and it immediately convinced Peter and his companions and subsequently the Jerusalem church.

(c) When the twelve Ephesians were baptized in the Holy Spirit, they spoke in tongues and prophesied (Acts 19:1-7). Even here where two gifts are mentioned the order is significant. It was natural for Luke to record tongues first, for this was the customary evidence, and this was followed by the further gift of prophecy. Valuable though prophecy is, there is no scriptural indication that it ever replaced tongues as the initial evidence of having received the Spirit, for, as we shall see later, prophecy was manifested in Bible times quite apart from and prior to the Spirit's coming at Pentecost. It is sufficient at this point to say that prophecy is never mentioned in isolation at the time of Spirit baptism, it is not mentioned again in connection with Spirit baptism, and here where prophecy is found in such a context it follows tongues.

It is highly significant that within these three groups there was probably a total of at least 160 people[2] and every one of them spoke in tongues when they received the Spirit. Consequently, the universal pattern is more evident than if there had only been three or four people in each group and these had all spoken in tongues.

2. Speaking in tongues is not explicitly mentioned when the Samaritans received the Spirit, but it can be deduced from what the narrative did record.

(a) Simon had already witnessed signs, great miracles, healings and deliverance in Philip's ministry prior to the time the Samaritan believers received the Spirit, and these effects had amazed him (see Acts 8:6-7, 13). But it was only later when he watched Peter and John pray with laying on of hands for the believers to receive the Spirit that he saw something different from that which he had seen before. Although the other signs through Philip had impressed him, it was the ability to bestow the Holy Spirit with this particular supernatural manifestation when he in turn laid hands on people which he now wanted to purchase. Clearly he had observed something from God that was new, arresting, and apparently beneficial. If Simon could dispense this gift in the same way, he would be really popular, for it was obviously a very real blessing to the people concerned. Tongues fits these criteria more than any other manifestation.

(b) In support of this we note that Simon must have seen something in the realm of God-inspired utterance, for after Peter had soundly rebuked him, Simon knew that though the others were speaking in the will of God he was excluded from such a gift: he had neither part nor lot in the *logos*, the speaking in which others were engaged (see v. 21).[3]

(c) If the Samaritans did in fact speak in tongues when they received the Spirit, it would parallel the evidence for tongues that we have already found at Pentecost, Caesarea and Ephesus where tongues were given without exception to each Christian.

(d) The absence of an explicit reference to tongues can be readily explained in the light of other references to the gift. When a recurring experience becomes the norm, there is no need to keep repeating a detailed description of it.

Harold Horton writes that "God gives us three detailed and well-authenticated reports of the baptism having been received with the supernatural evidence of tongues. He then expects us to have learned what to expect at subsequent baptisms and how they can be identified, authenticated and checked as complete. When Peter recounts to the brethren at Jerusalem the astonishing fact that the Gentiles at Caesarea had received the baptism in the Holy Spirit, 'the like gift as He gave unto us' (Acts 11:15-17; 15:8), *he does not repeat that they spoke with tongues.* The record of the actual event in Acts 10 includes both the baptism and its inseparable evidence, tongues. Peter now recounts the experience and *expects his brethren to infer the supernatural sign without his mentioning it.*

"It is not necessary to keep repeating in the record the details of any repeated blessing of the grace of God to the saved sinner. It is not recorded that the Philippian jailer either repented or was born again. It is simply reported that he believed on the Lord Jesus Christ and was thus saved. Paul knew all about the new birth, and, of course, the jailer could not be saved without being born again. That also Paul knew, and God the Recorder too. But the fact that it is not recorded that he was born again does not cast doubt either on the need or the fact of his new birth.

"God has given us in certain typical chapters of the Bible clear teaching on certain doctrines and experiences of salvation. For instance, the new birth is clearly set forth in John's Gospel and Peter's Epistle, and other scriptures. The essential of redeeming blood is set forth in Leviticus and Hebrews, and many other places. But there is no need repeatedly to mention the new birth or redeeming blood in every record of salvation. If Nicodemus must be born again in order to enter the kingdom of heaven, so must the Philippian jailer, whether his new birth is recorded or not.

"You would not say that Lydia was not washed in the blood of the Lamb because there is no record in scripture of the fact. Neither would you dare to claim that Lebbaeus whose surname was Thaddaeus was not baptized in water because there is no mention of the incident in the inspired record. And though it is recorded that the Ethiopian Eunuch was baptized in water it is not recorded that he was wet all over as the evidence of it as he emerged from the waters; but it would be unreasonable to declare or suppose that he was not. The inference in each of these instances is so unmistakable as to amount to a positive certainty. So is the inference that they spoke with tongues at Samaria."[4]

These words are relevant also to Paul's experience which we are about to consider. Yet before we do so, it may be helpful at this point to recall something we noticed in the previous chapter, that, where there is no mention of the Holy Spirit being initially received there is no mention of tongues being received either. Conversely, the only pattern which God has left us on the subject shows that wherever the reception of the Spirit is actually described, speaking in tongues is either explicitly or implicitly joined with it.

3. Paul almost certainly spoke in tongues when initially filled with the Spirit.

(a) As we have seen earlier, fullness of the Spirit refers to a fullness of inspiration and/or enablement. Therefore we could expect the fullness to be manifested in some supernatural way.

(b) Although Luke does not mention it, we know from Paul's open letter to the Corinthians that he spoke in tongues, so we are not crediting Paul with an experience for which we have no record. This experience obviously had a beginning either when he was baptized in the Spirit or at some later time.

(c) The most logical time for Paul to begin speaking in tongues would be when he was baptized in the Spirit. After Paul's conversion on the Damascus road, Ananias had placed his hands on him and prayed that he would receive his sight and "be filled with the Holy Spirit" (Acts 9:17-18). Although Luke does not stop to say so, we are clearly meant to infer that Ananias' prayer for fullness was answered. And if Paul was filled with the Spirit and spoke in tongues at the same time, this would be consistent with the experience not only of the other *apostles* who had all spoken in tongues at their Spirit baptism, but of early Christians generally.

(d) This conclusion is confirmed in an interesting insight that we are later given into Paul's method of ministry. In this we see him laying his hands upon new Ephesian believers just as Ananias had earlier done with him, and he did not leave until he had seen them baptized in the Spirit with speaking in tongues (Acts 19:1-7). It is certain that Ananias would have been equally unsatisfied if Paul had manifested anything less.

(e) We know that there were additional factors surrounding Paul's personal Pentecost which Luke found unnecessary to record in Acts 9:17-18. We find, for example, that Paul later alluded to his conversion and associated infilling with the Spirit at the hands of Ananias, although the human instrument God used is not mentioned by name (see Titus 3:5-6). In this passage Paul borrowed language reminiscent of the original pentecostal outpouring and showed that the same rich language aptly described subsequent receptions of the Spirit as well. He and Titus, like early Christians in general, had not only *received* the Spirit: they had received Him and been introduced to life in the Spirit *in a rich and memorable way*. The historic setting for this inundation could, of course, vary from Christian to Christian, but Paul could be assured that each Christian had experienced this abundant, copious outpouring of the Spirit (*execheen . . . plousiōs*). In Paul's case this had obviously occurred when, by divine command, Ananias had prayed for him to be filled with the activating and inspiring Breath of God.

Considered in isolation, any of the above factors may seem unconvincing, but their cumulative effect carries very considerable weight.

We can say, therefore, that it was quite unnecessary for Luke to state specifically that Paul was actually filled with the Spirit in answer to Ananias' prayer, or that Paul *ever* spoke in tongues, or that Paul's experience at his infilling was a rich and memorable one. These were gaps in the narrative that Luke assumed his readers could fill in for themselves in the light of early Church practice and common sense. This was because the rich experience of receiving the Spirit and speaking in tongues was the regular pattern and such common knowledge that it was quite unnecessary to repeat the ever-recurring details. If Luke had expanded his account he would have mentioned the answer to Ananias' prayer for fullness and the evidence of that answer. In view of these factors it is clear that the most likely time for Paul to begin to speak in tongues was at his baptism in the Spirit.

4. A further reason for regarding tongues as the initial evidence that the believer has received the Spirit is found in the essential nature of the gift. Today, as in the early Church, the Spirit-baptized receive tongues first because by its very nature it puts God first. It is directed toward God: is involved with God: its environment is God: it consolidates the relationship between man and God.

When we receive the Holy Spirit we appreciate even more the meaning of our Lord's words concerning Him: "He will bear witness to me" and "He will glorify me, for he will take what is mine and declare it to you" (John 15:26; 16:14). This is exactly what He does. He makes Jesus more real to us, fixes our eyes on Him and His glory; shows us the wonder of His person—His love, saviorhood, lordship, preeminence, reality—and increases our love for Him. In addition, we become more fully aware of God as "Father" (Rom. 8:15-16). And with this revelation He gives tongues of praise with which to glorify Him. Like the early Christians there is the praising of God in the Spirit (1 Cor. 14:16), "speaking in tongues and extolling God," and "expressing the mighty works of God" (Acts 10:46; 2:11). The gift of tongues therefore presents not a contrast to glorifying Christ and the Father but a supernatural means of doing so.[5] The sign of speaking in tongues is a sign of the praying man.

Evangelism and Christian service in all its forms are the expressed will of God, but if these come before *Him* our priorities are wrong. It is still man's chief end to glorify God and enjoy Him forever. God must receive the firstfruits of our devotion, not just that which is left after others have been served (e.g., Ex. 22:29; 23:19; Lev. 23:10-11; Prov. 3:9; Matt. 6:33; Mark 12:29-31; 2 Cor. 8:5; Acts 13:2). Prophecy and other revelatory gifts are very valuable but they are centered more upon ministering to others. That is their great strength but also their great limitation. However, the gift of tongues is unique in that it is directed Godward and expresses our adoration, thanksgiving, praise and prayer as inspired and enabled by the Spirit. It is true that when we do this *we* are built up and better able to minister to *others*. Nonetheless, the primary object of our devotion is God himself, then mankind—and in that order.

It is not therefore a coincidence or a purely arbitrary decision on God's part to choose tongues as the first expression of the Spirit's outpouring upon a life. Instead it accords with the whole biblical revelation from the creation of Adam to the last pages of Revelation that our relationship with God must come first, and the firstfruits of our lives, service, harvest, devotion and income are His. Through the gift of tongues we give God first place in our service. We minister to and enrich Him. Not only we but He too is blessed by this expression of our love and faith (1 Cor. 14:16). Then as a result of putting Him first, any additional supernatural manifestations that follow will be subject to His greater control.

This is one of the strongest possible confirmations that we are right to see speaking in tongues as the initial evidence of the gift of the Spirit, for when a man is immersed in God's Holy Spirit he becomes first and foremost occupied with his Lord, and the gift becomes not only valuable but a necessary expression of this new spiritual dimension. He has drunk deeply of God's Spirit (see John 7:37-39; 1 Cor. 12:13), and as a result his whole concept of the greatness of salvation has enlarged. God himself becomes more real, and with this new Spirit-given enlightenment only the gift of speaking in tongues can express the worshipper's adoration directly to Him. And as it is expressed at that time it becomes an obvious and objective testimony to his baptism in the Holy Spirit. In other words, because only an immersion in the Spirit can release such a new Spirit-inspired language of praise and worship to God, it becomes the immediate and convincing supernatural evidence or sign of this profound encounter with Him.

Once it is recognized on the basis of the above passages that speaking in tongues accompanies the act of receiving the Holy Spirit, it is little wonder that Christians find in both the following texts further clues as to the reason why God made it so.

(a) When there is an inflooding of the Spirit there will be a deep vocal expression, for it is a fact of life that whether the heart is filled with good or evil, "out of the abundance of the heart the mouth speaks" (Matt. 12:34). In Spirit baptism God fills, floods, releases, and uses men for His praise and glory, and nothing can express that abundance as adequately as tongues.

(b) Of all the members of the human body, the tongue is the most difficult to subdue. "No human being can tame the tongue; [it is] a restless evil, full of deadly poison" (see James 3:6-8). So often it is the main thing that obstructs the freedom of the Holy Spirit in a believer's life. Through our speech we express our individuality and the all too ready determination to manage our own affairs and to say what suits us personally. Little wonder then that the tongue has the power to pollute ourselves and others. Yet when the Church can see that the Holy Spirit is controlling the very organ which we could not ourselves control and is inspiring it with supernatural speech for His glory, it is a beautiful indication that a very profound transaction has taken place. Speaking in tongues under divine control thus becomes an apt testimony to such an invasion by the Spirit.

Before we leave this section it is interesting to notice that in the generations immediately following the death of the last original apostle this same New Testament pattern continued. Irenaeus, for example, described the *teleioi* (complete, mature, perfect) as "those who have received the Spirit of God and who through the Spirit of God do speak in all languages."[6] This is not scripture, of course, and we do not therefore draw doctrine from it, but it does demonstrate that even in Irenaeus' own lifetime, far from considering it foreign, the Christian Church still recognized that the particular manifestation of speaking in languages (tongues) was bound up with receiving the Spirit.

9

Suggested Alternative Signs and Related Questions

The belief that speaking in tongues is the initial sign indicating believers have been baptized in the Spirit is firmly grounded in Scripture. There are, however, various other ideas and gifts which have been suggested as validating evidence of Spirit baptism, and we now turn our attention to these and other related questions.

A Look at Alternatives

"*We accept by faith that when we were converted we automatically received the Holy Spirit and we need no evidence at all to be assured that we were then baptized in the Spirit.*"

We have already seen in the first chapter that baptism in the Spirit was not automatic upon saving faith, or upon saving faith and baptism. We saw too that it was a blessing immediately perceptible, and it is obvious that Simon the magician was not the kind of person to offer money for the ability to produce some invisible effect! (Acts 8:14-19). Clearly there was no room in the early Church for the "accept-the-Spirit-by-faith-without-evidence" attitude. By faith, yes, but the faith that appropriated the Holy Spirit was not alone: faith *received* a definite convincing manifestation of the Spirit's coming, and received it immediately.

"*The fruit of the Spirit, and love in particular, is the evidence of being baptized in the Spirit.*"

The fruit of the Spirit and holiness of life are imperative as we have already stressed. It is a serious matter if this fruit is not growing. In no way do we disregard it. Yet although love is an essential part of Christian living, the Church did not regard it as evidence of having received the Spirit. Fruit takes time to develop and become evident under various testings, and there was no such waiting period for development and assessment in the early Church (Acts 2:1-4; 8:14-18; 10:44-47; 19:1-6). The Old Testament saints and many others loved the Lord yet were *never* baptized in the Spirit. The 120 disciples, the Samaritans and the Ephesians loved the Lord *before* they were baptized in the Spirit. It would therefore be quite unwarranted to claim that love and character signified that Spirit baptism had occurred, for it had not.

"*The test of whether people had received the Holy Spirit was seen in the 3000 new believers, not in tongues or supernatural manifestations which are not even mentioned, but by submitting to divine teaching, fellowshipping together, partaking of the Lord's Supper, and praying (Acts 2:41-42). This corresponds with the three tests which the apostle John mentions in his letter. These were the signs that a Christian had been baptized in the Spirit.*"

(1) It is foolish to assume that the 3000 did not speak in tongues because the gift was not mentioned, for, as we have seen before, if silence decides the issue we must say that they had also neither repented nor received the Spirit, since these are also unrecorded. This view is as illogical as claiming that apart from the exceptions of the first disciples and the time when an apostle was present at Troas (Acts 20:7-11), no converts described in Acts ever submitted to divine teaching, fellowshipped together, partook of the Supper and prayed, because nowhere is such a description given of them.

(2) The three tests which John lists, namely, righteousness of life, brotherly love, and faith in Jesus as God incarnate (1 John 2:3-11, 23; 3:3, 23-24), are tests by which a Christian could discriminate between the true and the false—between genuine Christians and heretics. John's letter therefore presents the very basic signs of divine *life* and tests by which a person could be assured of salvation in Jesus Christ. Nowhere does John imply that he was describing how to recognize whether new disciples had been baptized in the Spirit.

(3) It is a fallacy to argue that these were tests of Holy Spirit baptism, for it would mean that the 120 disciples would have passed, or had the spiritual capacity to pass, all the tests *before* Pentecost and prior to their baptism in the Spirit! They are therefore effective tests of being regenerate, but not of Spirit baptism.

(4) We do not, in any case, have to decide between gifts and any of the above factors listed in Acts 2:41-42 and 1 John. For

example, the 120 spoke in tongues and *also* submitted to divine teaching, fellowshipped together, partook of the Supper and prayed. While Luke does not say so, none would dispute that the Samaritans, Cornelius, his household, the Ephesians and others would have done the same. We too should not think we must choose between tongues or these other evidences of divine life, but recognize that they belong together.

"*The initial evidence of baptism in the Spirit is power for service, for Jesus said: 'You shall receive power when the Holy Spirit has come upon you; and you shall be my witnesses . . .' (Acts 1:8).*"

It would lead to completely unwarranted conclusions if an apparently successful ministry was believed to indicate that a person had received the Holy Spirit. Jonah, for example, was instrumental in the repentance of a huge city (Jonah 3:1 10), but there was, of course, no baptism in the Spirit or promise of the Father realized before Pentecost.

We wholeheartedly endorse that baptism in the Spirit is followed by a distinct supernatural release of spiritual power. This really happens. The Spirit is given to enable every Christian to become a living demonstration and witness of Jesus' power in the world. As we have already noted, however, this power was seen initially among the early Christians in the ability to glorify Jesus supernaturally in tongues, and to bear their own individual and supernatural witness in the midst of other Christians (Acts 2:4; 8:14-18; 10:44-48; 19:1-7). It was only after this that the powerful witness to their love for Christ was made before non-Christians (e.g., Acts 2:5-13). Peter's challenging message to the crowd was to be greatly used in witnessing to others about the Lord, but *before* this he had been praising Him in tongues (Acts 2:14-41). To say this is in no way to minimize the absolute importance of evangelism but to show the historic order in which the promise of power was fulfilled.

"*On the Day of Pentecost wind and fire signified that people had been baptized in the Spirit. This supports the view that ANY supernatural evidence would suffice as evidence of receiving the Spirit.*"

Clearly, however, wind and fire did not indicate that the Holy Spirit had been given.

(1) When wind and fire occurred in the Old Testament they

dramatically signified the divine presence, but not, of course, Spirit baptism, which is confined to the New Covenant. God reserved a new and unique sign for a new and unique event.

(2) On the Day of Pentecost the wind and fire *preceded* the disciples' baptism, whereas speaking in tongues was a *consequence* of the baptism.

(3) Baptism in the Spirit with speaking in tongues was possible only because the disciples surrendered themselves physically, mentally, spiritually and vocally to the Lord (*"They* spoke in tongues . . ."). In other words, the God-given ability to speak in tongues, by its nature, indicated God's deep inflooding work in man, and man's willing response to His initiative. Wind and fire, on the other hand, were external to the disciples. They were a sign of God's presence, not a sign of the disciples' response. They signified God alone in action, whereas tongues signified God and man acting together. On the Day of Pentecost the disciples did not of course "receive" or "manifest" the wind and fire, but they did personally receive and manifest speaking in tongues. Tongues, though inspired, had become *their* act.

(4) There are no further references to wind and fire in connection with baptism in the Spirit.

(5) Even on the Day of Pentecost wind and fire were manifest in addition to tongues: they were not substitutes for tongues. Each had its own separate meaning.

It is clear therefore that wind and fire were regarded as awesome signs of the Lord's presence at the descent of the Holy Spirit and the inauguration of the New Covenant. They were never signs of baptism in the Holy Spirit.

"Prophecy, visions and dreams can be signs of baptism in the Holy Spirit, for Joel and Peter linked them with the Spirit's outpouring (see Joel 2:28-29; Acts 2:17-18)."

(1) Prophecy, visions and dreams are all found frequently in the Old Testament, and within the New Testament are linked with Joseph, Zechariah, Caiaphas, Pilate's wife, Saul and Cornelius (Matt. 1:20; 27:19; Luke 1:67; John 11:49-51; Acts 9:3-6; 10:3-7), yet in none of these cases did they signify Spirit baptism. The experience of Cornelius, for example, demonstrates that divinely given revelation can occur in the Christian age even before conversion, let alone Spirit baptism.

(2) Joel and Peter were not stating that the moment a person was baptized in the Spirit he would instantly prophesy or have

a vision or a dream, but rather that as a result of the new age which began with the outpouring of the Spirit, God's people would be inspired to prophesy,[1] see visions and dream dreams. There is nothing requiring us to believe that these would be the immediate and initial signs that individuals had received the Spirit.

(3) When on the Day of Pentecost Peter preached under a prophetic anointing, his message contained many truths which he could not have declared so authoritatively apart from revelation, but before that, he and 119 others had been worshipping the Lord in tongues.

(4) Nor do we find in the other accounts of Spirit baptism reference to prophecy, visions or dreams being given before those who had received the Spirit had spoken in tongues. *After* tongues, however, there was room for these as the Spirit inspired.

(5) It is certain, in any case, that private visions or dreams by their more subjective nature could not be as readily verified, and would therefore be unsuitable as an initial sign of Spirit baptism. Romans 8:9 requires some distinct objective sign which immediately gave convincing proof that the Spirit had in fact been received and that the recipients had therefore been accepted by the Lord and belonged to Him.

Nor were they stirring emotional experiences considered as evidence of the Spirit's coming, for believers could experience a wonderful and great sense of joy and excitement without being baptized in the Spirit (Matt. 28:8; Luke 24:52-53; Acts 8:8, 15-16).

Strong or unusual physical or spiritual sensations similarly did not qualify as initial evidence that people had been baptized in the Spirit. Nor did the gifts of the words of wisdom and of knowledge, faith, healing, working of miracles, prophecy and discernment of spirits, for these are also found in both Testaments among those who had not been Spirit baptized (e.g., 1 Kings 18:39; 2 Chron. 5:13-14; Jer. 20:9; 23:9; Acts 9:3-6; 10:3-7).

The same can be said for a glorious awe-inspiring sense of the Lord's immediate presence and reality, or sudden clarity in understanding the Scriptures. Wonderful though these can be, they presented no assurance of a personal pentecost, nor were they a substitute for it. The two on the Emmaus road saw the risen Lord and later said: "Did not our hearts burn within us while he talked to us upon the road, while he opened to us the scriptures?" Yet they had not at that time been baptized in the Holy Spirit (Luke 24:31-32; see also Acts 9:3-6).

Love, joy and the above attitudes or experiences could be very holy, genuine, and a wonderful indication that God had definitely met, anointed, blessed or ministered. But clearly these did not indicate that a believer had received the Spirit. If we stand on the scriptures alone, we have no option but to disregard them as initial evidence, for they and other suggestions like them do not accord with the biblical accounts of baptism in the Holy Spirit, and in any case, they can indicate something entirely different. It would be misleading and potentially impoverishing to regard these spiritual experiences as initial evidence of receiving the Spirit when Scripture is not only silent on their being such, but clearly presents a different pattern.[2]

What About Speaking in Tongues by Non-Christians?

Sometimes people question how Christians could ever consider tongues as evidencing Holy Spirit baptism when pagans and non-Christians have spoken in tongues that were obviously not inspired by the Spirit of God.

Christians who walk with God would not be deceived by counterfeit tongues, for some basic facts concerning true tongues preclude this. There are vast differences in a tongue originating from Satan and a tongue originating from God—a world of difference! We list some of them.

1. Unlike false tongues-speaking by pagans and non-Christians, the one who seeks to be baptized in the Spirit and speak in tongues believes in a holy God: Father, Son and Holy Spirit. He has repented of sin and trusts solely in the Lord Jesus Christ for salvation. Though very imperfect, he knows, loves and seeks to follow the Lord further. He has a hunger and thirst for more of Christ. He seeks a deeper relationship with Jesus the Baptizer in the Spirit. He is not a pagan, heathen or one involved in false religion, heresy, evil or immoral practices. To state the obvious, his prayer for the blessing of God upon his life is directed to the Lord, just as it was when he was seeking salvation in Christ. It is not made to Satan or to some vague unknown god.

2. True tongues are found within the general context and spiritual fellowship of other orthodox Christians. Although it is not necessary for them to be present with the seeker at the time of receiving, they, with him, believe that God's will on tongues has been made abundantly clear, and further believe that He delights to give good gifts to those who ask Him (see Luke 11:13; Matt. 7:11). When the tongues are manifested in answer to prayer

the gift is verifiable by these fellow Christians gathered together in Christ's name (Matt. 18:20).

3. When the Christian first speaks in tongues, even though his faith may be small, it is evident that he is worshipping, enjoying and speaking *to* God. True tongues uplifts the Father, and Christ the Savior, Lord and Baptizer.

4. The believer is fully in control of the true utterance. There is absolutely nothing ecstatic or uncontrolled about it. It stands in complete contrast to the false utterance. It takes no effort for a Christian to discern between the languages of a man of God and one who opposes the Christian faith in life and blasphemous utterance. Equally, with tongues the differences between true and false languages and their whole spirit and nature would be immediately apparent to the discerning.

These points add up to vast differences between the true and false. Nevertheless, because the issue is important, it is the church's loving responsibility to check out prayerfully any utterance. If, for example, a Christian had earlier been involved in occult activity and manifested a demonic tongue, ordinary discernment plus the gift of discerning of spirits is available. The Spirit could quickly be identified and cast out and the seeker then baptized in the Holy Spirit with a true gift of tongues that was entirely different from the former, and that testified to the Spirit's rich outpouring. (We will return to the subject of the counterfeit in chapter eleven.)

The differences, then, are so pronounced that the apostles did not need to spell them out.

Is This Not Too Restrictive?

Other Christians ask a different question: "Is it not too restrictive to regard speaking in tongues as the initial scriptural evidence of baptism in the Spirit, for the Spirit of God blows where He wills?"

In answer we would point out that God restricts himself. There is only one God. He has given us only one Book as the basis for faith and practice. Only through shedding of blood is there remission of sins. Salvation is restricted to only one way—through Jesus Christ the only Savior. Only by new birth is salvation possible. Baptism is the only sacrament of initiation described and commanded by the Lord.

In these and many other ways God restricts himself and His Church.

Baptism in the Spirit and speaking in tongues is not the end of the road but the beginning of life in a new dimension. After the initial expression worship in tongues will continue, but now there is, of course, scope for a wide variety of gifts and graces as God leads out in new service in His name.

Jesus and Tongues

Some people argue that speaking in tongues has minimal importance and cannot be the initial sign, since Jesus, they say, did not speak in tongues when baptized in the Spirit or at any other time. At least four things can be said in reply:

1. After the Spirit's descent upon Jesus He was said to be *full* of the Spirit. He was now inspired, anointed and enabled for His public ministry. It is not said, however, that this was when He *received* the Spirit or was *baptized* in the Spirit, and it is surely wrong to confuse it with such. As we have noticed in an earlier chapter, people could be filled (inspired) with the Spirit prior to Pentecost without being Spirit-baptized. Because Jesus was perfect and divine it could be that He had no need to be baptized in the Spirit at all (or at least not in the sense that Christians are initiated into life in the Spirit), and had no need to receive an additional prayer gift. We should not, therefore, assume that the absence of tongues in the account of Jesus' *infilling* parallels our own *baptism* in the Spirit.

2. Even if Jesus did not speak in tongues, this cannot indicate that Christians should not, for He by the Spirit inspired them to do so (Acts 2:33; 1 Cor. 12:5). He obviously knew it had real value and purpose for His followers. Their earlier request, "Lord, teach *us* to pray" (Luke 11:1) was now being answered in a new way.

3. Jesus may not have spoken in tongues because His perfect relationship with His Father may have made the gift unnecessary. Not so for us, however. We are not sinless as was the Lord. We cannot say with Him, "I and the Father are one" (John 10:30), or, "I always do what is pleasing to the Father" (John 8:29). He therefore never needed to confess sins, or ask for light or the power to consecrate himself more perfectly, but it is right for us to do so. If Jesus did not speak in tongues, it may have been because, unlike us, He had no need to be built up spiritually.

4. Yet we should be wary of assuming that Jesus did not speak in tongues. As Thomas Smail says, "The personal prayer life of Jesus is covered with a veil of almost unbroken reticence,

so that no conclusion about the possible place of tongues in it can, one way or the other, be drawn."[3] Some have suggested that the word *stenazein*, used of our Lord's "sighing" or "groaning," was a technical term for prayer which did not involve the mind, but was called forth by the Spirit (Mark 7:34; 8:12).[4] That may or may not be so. Yet even if we disregard this possibility, we do know that much was said in the secret place of which we are ignorant (e.g., Mark 1:35; Luke 6:12; Matt. 6:6). When in the unshadowed intimacy of His private communion with the Father, Jesus wanted to express all the depth and fullness of His own spirit, and there were no Aramaic (or Greek) words suitable, it would seem incredible if this had to go unsaid. Surely there were many times of sublime intimate fellowship between God the Father and God the Son when limited human language must have utterly failed, and when some unrestricted language of the spirit was required to express all that was in His heart.[5] If this language was not tongues, it would seemingly have to be something closely akin to it.

This does not of course prove that Jesus spoke in tongues. It does, however, establish the possibility, even probability, that during His earthly life, and well before the Spirit's descent, Jesus prayed in the Spirit in a heavenly language which transcended the severely restricted language of men.

Regardless, however, of whether Jesus spoke in tongues, His life presents no obstacle to the view that after Pentecost the initial proof of Spirit baptism was speaking to the Lord in tongues.

What of Fine Christians Who Never Spoke in Tongues?

Another argument is sometimes advanced: "We know that there are indications that some great men like Charles Finney, D. L. Moody and others may well have spoken in tongues. But what about great servants of God like R. A. Torrey, Andrew Murray, F. B. Meyer, Hudson Taylor and a host of other wonderful Christians who apparently never spoke in tongues? They evidently did not need the gift so why should we? And were they not baptized in the Spirit?"

This question is akin to another: "If God uses the Salvation Army which practices neither baptism nor the Lord's Supper, does this not demonstrate that these two sacraments must, after all, be quite irrelevant today? We can therefore jettison them without real loss!"

It is immediately obvious that arguments such as these are not based upon the Bible but rather upon what men have or have not done over recent centuries of Church history. As such they may be interesting questions to debate but they are severely limited in value. The Church is built solely upon the foundation of the apostles and prophets with Christ himself as the chief cornerstone (Eph. 2:20). Thus the words of Jesus given personally or through these inspired men provide the foundation and the norm for whatever we do or teach. We can gain much by reading of the experiences of other Christians, as long as we remember that there is a fundamental difference between following Jesus Christ and His inspired apostles and prophets, and following His more recent followers.

The short answer to questions like these is the same as that given after Peter asked the Lord where his friend John fitted into the Savior's plans. "What is that to you?" Jesus answered; "*you* follow me" (see John 21:19-22). Our Lord was saying: "Peter, it is more important that you get your eyes off others and on to me. Forget how others do or don't follow me. They are my business, not yours! They are not the standard of what I want *you* to be. You be concerned to follow in the way I reveal to you. Don't let your curiosity about others rob you of my best for you, but concentrate instead on what *I* want in your life."

If we start comparing Christian with Christian to try to find our standards for salvation, baptism, Spirit baptism or anything else, we will deserve to be confused and misled into accepting less than God's will (2 Cor. 10:12). Yet rather than having us arguing for some mediocre or diminished level of Christian experience, God desires to bring us into full New Testament richness.

Even if it could be established that these successful men had definitely not spoken in tongues, it would not prove that this was God's perfect plan for them; neither would it prove that they would not have been much more effective had they spoken in tongues. It would be equally futile to seek to validate or prove our own theological conclusions from the fact that other men of God such as Tommy Hicks and many others did in fact speak in tongues and were used by the Lord in a truly phenomenal way.[6]

There may be many interesting questions concerning these matters which we would like answered fully and clearly. But regardless of whether we get explanations which satisfy us, our task is still to follow the Lord and be guided by His Word. If we do not do this, then for all our claims, our own and others' experience along with Church history and evangelical tradition becomes the standard of faith and practice to which we finally submit, rather than the Scriptures alone.

We can, however, make some observations on the above question.

We should bear in mind that even in the Old Testament there were many great saints who were fine, disciplined and dedicated servants of God who walked with Him, heard His voice and saw major results from their ministry. There was even a most reluctant prophet like Jonah who saw what could be interpreted as outstanding success (Jonah 3:1-10). Yet none of these qualities or their effectiveness were signs that they had been baptized in the Holy Spirit, for the Spirit's outpouring was anticipated but unrealized under the Old Covenant.

Concerning the particular people mentioned in the question we are considering, we gladly acknowledge that God anointed and used these great men and we honor them and thank God for them. They have enriched the whole Church. We rejoice that God has used many people who have a different form of baptism from our own, or even no form of baptism or the Lord's Supper at all, who have a different liturgy, or whose views on some aspects of the faith differ from our own. Though there may be these differences, we are not claiming that we are superior to them, for in various ways they may have been better stewards than we are.

Yet it is humanistic and futile to fasten on any non-apostolic period, personality or group in the life of the Church and allow it to become the standard of principle and practice, of right and wrong. In such ways we can easily make void the Word of God by our traditions, and effectively replace the biblical patterns and teaching with those which have greater human appeal. We then agree with the Bible only if the Bible agrees with us!

These same Christians accomplished what they did because the past standards of Christianity did not anchor them. Instead they were determined to trust and follow the Lord the best way they knew. They would have been alarmed to think future generations would limit God's work to the level of truth an earlier generation had experienced, for they would have been the first to say all truth did not rest with them. They would willingly acknowledge their imperfection and bias to human tradition, and would not limit us just as we would not limit others to our level of understanding. We also would like future Christians to progress well beyond the truths we have appropriated, for anyone baptized in the Spirit is keenly aware that he has not reached an ultimate standard.

Over recent centuries there has been an ongoing recovery of truth as God has progressively revealed the significance of scriptures relating to justification by faith alone, baptism, the need for evangelical missions, personal holiness, social concern, the ministry of every believer in the Church, and baptism in, and the continuing ministry of, the Holy Spirit. As God revealed truth to earlier generations they were required to live up to it, and when they did God abundantly blessed them and their ministries. Each of these great Christians strongly opposed the view that at conversion a Christian receives all. They preached (quite aggressively!) the need for, and had personally experienced, a further work of grace which they called baptism with the Spirit, though to our knowledge these particular men never said they spoke in tongues.

Yet some of them may well have spoken in tongues without making it known. This is not as farfetched as it may appear. Some Christians even over recent and more tolerant decades have stated that they were speaking in tongues for years but did not mention it because it would be widely misunderstood and rejected, and in the prevailing religious climate their own Christian service would be curtailed. Even until relatively recently there was much misunderstanding with false accusations, innuendo, heresy charges, excommunication or removal from ministry, and attacks from leaders and writers who had no personal understanding of such gifts. Where a church insisted that gifts had ceased with the death of the apostles or with the completion of the canon, then in line with its own criteria it had no option but to expose any persisting gifts and reject them as counterfeit![7] In such a climate it would not be surprising if some Christian leaders did not volunteer that they prayed in tongues.

We cannot be dogmatic when we can read what are at best only very incomplete accounts of the lives of these men, and when we cannot question them about their experiences and private prayer times. In such circumstances we can only say that without doubt these people had genuine and deep encounters with the Lord. If they had in fact received the gift of speaking to the Lord in tongues, that would mean they were baptized in the Spirit in the way scripture describes, and brought into a completely new dimension of supernatural worship and service. If on the other hand they had definitely *not* received this ability, their deep and rich encounter with the Lord for all its strength and reality still lacked the full richness and completeness of New Testament baptism in the Spirit. Although the experience they called Holy Spirit baptism contained many true features of such a baptism, it still lacked some very significant, important and unique qualities. The connection of Holy Spirit baptism with the supernatural was something they apparently either did not see, or if they did, did not recognize that this was still God's will and available to them. To say this is neither to dishonor them nor to claim that we are superior, but rather to acknowledge that there was greater enrichment in God and an added supernatural dimension of baptism in the Spirit (and fullness of the Spirit) of which they had little or no personal knowledge.

Needless to say, people today can similarly have deep and rich encounters with the Lord but still lack some rich and significant aspects of New Testament baptism in the Spirit. Even those who believe that it is permissible to regard this theologically as "baptism in the Spirit," though without tongues, can find *in Scripture* no other initial sign than that of speaking to the Lord in a divinely given gift of tongues.

Summary of Biblical Evidence

It is abundantly clear that early Christians received the Holy Spirit with definite observable supernatural evidence of His presence. Furthermore, there is very strong evidence for the belief that this supernatural accompaniment was always in the form of speaking to the Lord in tongues, and that by the presence or absence of this gift Christians could know whether the Spirit had or had not been received.

Such a belief is supported by (1) the actual biblical records of baptism in the Holy Spirit where tongues are explicit or implied, (2) the nature of the gift of tongues which focuses on God, addresses Him, and offers Him the firstfruits of the Spirit's outpouring, (3) the fact that tongues—which are for every Christian[8]—must be received some time and Spirit baptism is the obvious time, and (4) the inadequacy of all other suggested alternative forms of evidence by which Christians immediately knew that believers had in fact been baptized in the Spirit.

Those who challenge this belief and teach that there was other initial evidence of having been baptized in the Spirit in New Testament times are obliged by logic to show from Scripture what that evidence was which instantly convinced the early Christians that the Spirit had in fact just been received.

Therefore, numerous lines of evidence establish that in the New Testament, the first clear indication of the sudden, rich, full outpouring which is baptism in the Spirit, was speaking in tongues, or, to elaborate, praising and worshipping Jesus and the Father in a new Spirit-inspired language. Only this sign does full justice to the scriptural record which the Lord has left for our guidance. Yet this supernatural manifestation is not the end but the beginning, for while continuing to pray in tongues this gift must be followed in the longer term by other evidences of growth in grace and in knowledge of the Lord.

Are Exceptions Possible?

Although Scripture indicates that tongues always accompanied Spirit baptism in the early Church, one remaining question calls for our attention. In contrast to the early Christians, how do we regard the modern Christian who has had a profound experience of the Spirit and as a result immediately finds himself initiated into a distinct realm of *supernatural* experience and ministry, but who does not speak in tongues until sometime later? This happens only occasionally (and then usually where no suitable ministries have been available, or where there have been negative influences regarding tongues), but it does happen!

There are two important points to take into account when looking at this question of exceptions.

1. Speaking in tongues is the only initial *scriptural* evidence of baptism in the Spirit. There is no other initial sign to which we can point in the New Testament.

2. God has reserved a unique place and purpose for tongues, and therefore any other manifestation accompanying Spirit baptism must of necessity lack some very rich and significant qualities present in New Testament experience. However, where there is a progressive recovery of biblical truth it is possible that anomalies may sometimes occur, because the Church has been seriously confused over many points concerning Christian initiation, and has frequently neither taught nor acted as in apostolic times. (It has certainly not been as eager as were the apostles to complete Christian initiation where any element has been lacking.) Therefore, in returning to the New Testament pattern, allowance should probably be made for the possibility that occasionally a person may be "baptized in the Spirit" without the scriptural accompaniment of speaking to the Lord in tongues. Yet even here, Spirit baptism will, as its name implies, involve a profound encounter with the Spirit, and, because it is the occasion of infilling with the Spirit,[9]

it will be marked by definite supernatural manifestations, which, because of their obvious truth and continuing nature, provide an authenticating witness, both to the candidate and onlookers, that a profound new spiritual dimension has been entered. Speaking in tongues would then follow as a consequence of Spirit baptism.

The danger of making this point is that people can rationalize and see themselves as the exception to the consistent way God acted in New Testament times—and they may even be proud of being an exception! (Many, of course, may think themselves exceptions when they have simply not been baptized in the Spirit at all. And we recall that even though non-Christians are obviously without the Spirit, God sometimes manifested prophecy through them.) However, even if you consider yourself an exception, it is your privilege and responsibility to enter into your full biblical and Christian inheritance by seeking God for His gift of tongues. Then the deficiency is supplied and your experience and relationship with Him is normalized.

The gift of tongues is not to be thought of as if it was something to avoid, as if it represented some nasty aspect in God's dealings, as if He just could not help giving the bad with the good. (How such attitudes dishonor the Lord and question His love and wisdom!) Neither is it some nebulous or self-directed gift without purpose, a miraculous gift without reason for being. Speaking in tongues is a wonderful and holy gift of a loving Father who wants to release, bless, encourage and build up every one of His children as they cross the threshold of Holy Spirit baptism into life in the Spirit. It is a further expression of His boundless grace.

10

Is Speaking in Tongues the Least Important Gift?

It is often argued, because tongues are placed at the end of the list of gifts in 1 Cor. 12:28, that speaking in tongues is the least important, and time spent considering or exercising it is majoring on minors. Yet there are many reasons why it is impossible to accept this assumption.

The Evidence Surveyed

1. *Scripture nowhere says speaking in tongues is the least important gift.*

2. *Many valuable gifts are completely omitted from the list in 1 Cor. 12:28.* This list is obviously incomplete, for it contains no allusion at all to six of the nine gifts in 12:8-10. It would therefore be illogical to argue that *the missing gifts* were of lesser or no consequence. Obviously the 12:28 list was never intended to imply that any gift had the lowest place, or that any unlisted gift was therefore spurious or valueless.

3. *Only one list places tongues last.* Every list in which tongues is featured shows that it is last in only one of the six catalogues: it is the eighth in a list of nine (1 Cor. 12:8-10), eighth and last in an otherwise differently ordered list (12:28), sixth in a list of seven (12:29-30), first before prophecy, knowledge and faith (13:1-2), second in a list of three (13:8), fourth in a list of five (14:26).

4. *Paul refuses to distinguish narrowly between many of the gifts.* In 1 Cor. 12:28, after mentioning the first three offices (apostles, prophets, teachers) in what is probably their order of importance, Paul does not continue his "first, second, third," for he does not wish to distinguish narrowly between those who exercise the remaining gifts.

5. *The last-mentioned can be of major importance.* Whereas one list places tongues last, three (1 Cor. 12:8-10, 29-30; 14:26) place interpretation last, while three do not even mention interpretation (12:28; 13:1-2, 8). Yet we know that interpretation following tongues builds up the whole congregation to the same extent as prophecy (14:5). Interpretation—or interpreted tongues—is therefore in the very *highest* category of gifts in its edifying ability for the whole church.

6. *Tongues are enriching and commended.* Paul gives detailed teaching on tongues, emphasizes that it is a means of personal enrichment, commends it (1 Cor. 14:4-5), and does not want its correct exercise hindered (14:39).

7. *The position of other gifts contradicts the view that the gifts continue in a diminishing order of importance.* If, as is likely, "helpers" in 1 Cor. 12:28 refers to the work of deacons, while "administrators" refers to the service given by overseers or elders, then their position in the text also rules out the possibility that the gifts continue in a diminishing order of importance, for the function of deacon is certainly not greater than that of elder.

8. *Comparison with other lists argues against tongues being inferior.* By comparison, the fact that self control is the last-named fruit of the Spirit does not mean it is the least important. Love that is stressed in 1 Cor. 13, first in Gal. 5:22, fourth in 1 Tim. 6:11 is the last of the qualities mentioned in 2 Pet. 1:7. Again, it would be illogical to assume that in the lists in Acts 15:29, Eph. 4:11, 6:10-17 and 2 Pet. 1:5-7, the last is least important or unnecessary. There is difference but no thought of inferiority or superiority.

9. *Prophecy's position also shows that it is impossible to argue importance or nonimportance from its position in a list.* Paul regards prophecy as the highest gift to aim for, yet five gifts precede it in 1 Cor. 12:8-10. Its position neither illustrates its importance nor otherwise.

10. *No gift is to be despised or belittled.* The view that the gift of tongues is least and should be minimized, would contradict Paul's whole argument in 1 Cor. 12:15-20, where he discourages anyone saying, "I'm only a foot. I'm inferior. I'm at the very bottom of

the list." Paul would have none of this: "Your feet," he would say, "are essential members of the body, and if you despise or fail to use them the whole body suffers. It is not a matter of inferiority but variety. Your feet are needed for the perfect functioning of the body. Do not then despise *any* of God's gifts."

11. *God honors what man may consider unimportant.* Even if tongues had been last in each list, *God* has given "special honour to the humbler parts" (1 Cor. 12:24, NEB). Any argument that this is the least important, is, therefore, not only unwarranted but also purely academic, since God honors what men with their natural and limited understanding dishonor.

12. *Paul valued tongues highly.* Paul, an apostle—the office placed first in 1 Cor. 12:28—in private communion with God, practiced that which is at the end of that particular list, and did so more than any others!

13. *Tongues may be positioned among the last because they were given last.* In God's chronological order, tongues and interpretation were given last. The first seven gifts mentioned in 1 Cor. 12:28 are found in the Old Testament and in the Gospels, but these two were added in the Christian dispensation, the dispensation of the Spirit (see Heb. 8-10).

14. *Tongues may be positioned among the last because Paul wanted to discuss these newer gifts at depth.* Paul was about to give special instruction concerning tongues and interpretation, which were being abused. Therefore he mentions first the gifts that were no problem at Corinth, ending with those newer gifts on which he desired to elaborate.

15. *Its early reception and universal place among Christians argues for its importance.* Its universal place among all Christians at Jerusalem, Caesarea and Ephesus, where the reception of the Spirit is described, argues for its real importance in God's economy.

In view of these many factors, we certainly cannot say that the gift of tongues is of little importance or that it can be ignored. All the gifts are important. God has given each of them a special purpose. Speaking in tongues is *a gift from God.* To imply that it has little value for Christians or for Christ's Body is arrogant, and an insult to God's wisdom.

Jesus warned: "Whoever relaxes one of the *least* of these com-

mandments and teaches men so, shall be *called least* in the kingdom of heaven" (Matt. 5:19). When that can be said of an iota
or dot of the law and the prophets, we must also consider it ex-
ceedingly dangerous to minimize or disregard anything God gives
under the new and better covenant (see Heb. 7:22; 8:6-13; 12:24).
To regard any of the Spirit's gifts as least or of little consequence
or teach others so, inevitably results in a loss of sensitivity to His
Word and His will.

Each gift, including tongues, is best for the purpose and place
for which it was designed. So in worship within the Body of Christ,
tongues has its God-appointed place among all the other gifts. It
is to be controlled, but certainly not excluded, for with interpretation it is as valuable as prophecy. And it is also the only gift of
the Spirit for personal communion with God. No other gift has the
same unique features of prayer, praise, and personal upbuilding
for the individual Christian who uses it.

Is Speaking in Tongues the Most Spectacular Gift?

It may be helpful at this point to consider a somewhat related
question: *Is speaking in tongues the most spectacular gift?* Frequently those who can only be strangers to manifestations of the
Spirit assume that speaking in tongues was one of the most spectacular gifts, and that the Corinthians delighted in it for that reason. But acquaintance with the other gifts of power makes it clear
that tongues cannot be included at all among the more spectacular
manifestations.

For example, the following gifts are each more spectacular than
tongues: *Words of knowledge and of wisdom* which come directly,
exposing needs with information which only God could impart in
the circumstances, and which then minister edifying grace to those
same needs in a truly miraculous way; *the gift of faith* which releases powerful evidence of God's mighty hand; *gifts of healings*
of many kinds of deformity and sickness; *working of miracles*,
which is frequently linked with the gift of faith. Equally, *prophecy*
with its word direct from God, and *discernment of spirits* linked
as it is with bringing release to those Satan has bound, have an
obvious and profound effect.

To pray in tongues is therefore among the *least spectacular* of
the power gifts mentioned in 1 Cor. 12:8-10.

The Christian continues to speak in tongues, not because it is
the most spectacular but because in this unique way, by divine
enabling, he can communicate on the level of the spirit with his
Lord. This is every believer's privilege, open to him by faith.

11

Should Christians Seek Spiritual Gifts?

"It is wrong to seek a sign," someone suggests, *"for only a wicked and adulterous people do that. Since tongues and prophecy are signs we should therefore refrain from seeking them. If God wants us to have them they will be given without any seeking on our part, and if we do not receive them they are obviously not His will for us. Seeking of gifts is wrong, and it may well open the way to receiving a counterfeit."*

Another says: *"I have asked that God will give me anything that is His will, but as I have received no supernatural gifts in answer to my prayer they are evidently not for me, or at least not for me at this time."*

Are these lines of argument valid? I believe that they are not. We will consider the various issues involved in these objections:

"A wicked and adulterous people seek after a sign"

When Jesus spoke against seeking signs, He was addressing a specific audience of scribes, Pharisees and Sadducees (Matt. 12: 39; 16:4) who had seen the Messiah many times, had heard the words of God from His lips, and had already seen very many signs. *Further* signs would be useless to them since they had rejected light already given. Unlike the Ninevites they were not interested in repentance (Matt. 12:41). They were seeking signs but not truth; signs but not Him; signs not to confirm truth but to accuse Him (Luke 6:7, 11). No additional signs or miracles would help them. Nevertheless, one supreme and mighty sign would in fact be given when His Father raised Him from the dead after three days and vindicated Him before men.

Unlike the scribes and Pharisees, the Queen of Sheba spared no time, trouble and expense to listen to the words of wisdom given through Solomon. She eagerly absorbed everything that portrayed God's favor and blessing. And when she accepted them as signs of God's unmistakable activity, she responded in the best way she knew. But in sharp contrast and in spite of their increased privileges, the scribes and Pharisees rejected all the signs and wonders of the One immeasurably greater than Solomon.

If anyone *wills* to do God's will, he shall know the truth and see confirming evidences that God is at work. But if he will not believe, nothing will change him (John 7:17; 5:40), not even a miracle of resurrection (Luke 16:27-31). The evidence of the eyes alone is not sufficient to convince and give birth to faith, for faith is more than intellectual conviction: it also requires the surrender of heart and will to the Lord.

These warnings that Jesus gave to those who had repeatedly seen and rejected His message and power were not applied to those who had neither seen nor persistently rejected Him as Lord. Peter and John, who could hardly be termed "wicked and adulterous," were moved with compassion for a lame man and claimed a sign from God when they said to him: "In the name of Jesus Christ of Nazareth, walk." Instead of rejecting their prayer God responded to it, and many praised Him! (Acts 3:6; 4:21-22). But the very same sign annoyed the priests and Pharisees and they intensified their efforts to halt and discredit God's work. So Peter and John were arrested and brought before the council (Acts 4:1-3). Yet although these religious leaders could not deny the miracle and the weight of evidence, they refused to submit to the Lord (Acts 4:16-17).

Immediately after this Peter and John again sought signs when they prayed: "And now Lord. . . , allow us, your servants, to speak your message with all boldness. Stretch out your hand to heal, and grant that wonders and miracles may be performed through the name of your holy Servant Jesus" (Acts 4:29-30, TEV). Their request was positive and unashamed, and signs continued to accompany those who believed (Mark 16:17; Acts 2:22; Heb. 2:3-4; Rom. 15:17-19).

Although Jesus said that those who believe without seeing are more blessed, He graciously granted signs to sincere honest doubters to help them believe (John 20:24-29; Mark 9:24-25).

So the warning against seeking a sign was given to those who had been repeatedly confronted with the reality of His power and authority, heard His word and invitations—and yet rejected Him. His word is for those who demand a sign from the position of pure skepticism and unbelief yet have no intention of altering their attitudes, regardless of the marvels of love and compassion He performs all around them.

"Tongues and prophecy as signs"

The purpose of any gift has by no means been exhausted when we note that they are signs.

Jesus himself is described as *"a sign* that is spoken against," and He later said: *"As Jonah became a sign* to the men of Nineveh, *so will the Son of man be* to this generation" (Luke 2:34; 11:30).

Jesus certainly is a sign, but this is only one aspect of the teaching concerning Him, for He is infinitely more. He is also Son of God, Lord, Savior, Messiah, Prophet, Priest, King—and we could add a multiplicity of other titles. He himself invited people to *seek* Him—even though He is "a sign"—for rest, for living water, for the bread of life. These truths are so prominent that none should be troubled by the thought of seeking a sign when they seek Him. In the same way, we need so to appreciate the truths and benefits about tongues and prophecy that this mention of a sign similarly falls into perspective. We do not hesitate to seek Jesus, and neither should we hesitate to appropriate and experience spiritual gifts. *To be logical, people who are reluctant to seek gifts because they are a sign would need to refrain from seeking Jesus also since He too is described in this way.*

While speaking in tongues is a sign to unbelievers, it is a gift of prayer and praise to believers—inward, spiritual, constructive, and glorifying to the Lord. And while prophecy is a sign to believers it too is far more: it is a valuable gift of inspiration and revelation which brings spiritual strengthening to the Church.

We do not seek tongues or prophecy because they are signs but because they are spiritually constructive and bring glory and praise to Jesus our Lord.

"Why seek spiritual gifts when the Lord in His wisdom knows what is best for me?"

On the surface this attitude may seem valid, for it has the appearance of devotion and surrender to the will of God. Yet this is closer to non-Christian fatalism than to Christianity.

(a) Jesus himself encouraged children to *ask* their heavenly Father for the specific gift of the Holy Spirit, and for good gifts also, when He said: "If you then, who are evil, know how to give good gifts to your children, how much more will the heavenly Father give the Holy Spirit [and good things] *to those who ask him"* (Luke 11:13; Matt. 7:11). To ask for gifts that are readily available is therefore not presumption but an act of childlike trust and obedience which He commends.

(b) We have an apostolic directive to "earnestly desire" these spiritual gifts (1 Cor. 12:31; 14:1, 39). The verb translated "earnestly desire" or "strive" (*zéloō*) is a present imperative, a form which denotes a command to continue to do an action, or to do it repeatedly. We could well translate this as "keep on earnestly desiring . . ." or "continue to be zealous for spiritual gifts." The word *zéloō* which Paul uses here (as with the nouns *zélótés* and *zélos*), from which we get our words like "zealous" and "zealot," involves dedicated activity to reach the desired goal. Our Lord had an earnest desire (*zélos*) for His Father's house that made Him take drastic action (John 2:14-17). The Laodicean Christians were to be activated to repentance (Rev. 3:19). Saul was zealous in actively persecuting the Church (Phil. 3:6; Acts 22:3-4). A person cannot be "zealous for good deeds" (Titus 2:14) simply by sitting and praying that if it is God's will he will be given the opportunity to do good deeds. He must be actively taking all necessary steps. This apostolic command, then, cannot be understood passively, for it is impossible to be a passive or inactive zealot. A zealot cannot be resigned to the status quo!

It is significant that Paul addresses Christians who *already* have gifts of the Spirit operating in their lives (1 Cor. 1:5-7), and rather than suggest they now relax with what they have, he says: "It is imperative that you continue to be zealous for spiritual gifts."

This necessity of earnestly desiring and striving does not conflict with the Spirit apportioning gifts to each one individually as *He* wills (1 Cor. 12:11). His will concerning us is not an arbitrary one, but the *performing* of it depends upon our human desire and openness to receive from Him. Regardless of how much He wants to impart spiritual gifts to us, He will not do so unless His conditions are met. There must first be desire, capacity to receive, and the faith that knows God has promised and will perform His word (Heb. 6:12; Matt. 15:28). The hungry realize their need, yearn and partake of spiritual food, and are blessed as a result. But those who consider themselves already prosperous and requiring nothing further, become smug and contented, and cut themselves off from the proffered enrichment of God's grace (Rev. 3:16-20). Mary expressed the same truth when she said, "*He has filled the hungry with good things*"—and then follows the devastating phrase—"*and the rich he has sent empty away*" (Luke 1:53). Like his physical counterpart a spiritually hungry man is not easily put off! He will make every endeavor to get the spiritual blessing he craves, especially when he is sure his Father wants him to have it!

Jesus taught that eternal life is granted only to those to whom it is the Father's will to give it, but He also gave instruction to strive to enter in at the narrow gate. God has made earnest desire for the gift of His Son and the gift and gifts of His Spirit part of the receptive process, for unless there is this hunger and holy dissatisfaction, there is no real receiving. Jesus' own words were: "Blessed are those who hunger and thirst for righteousness, for *they* shall be satisfied" (Matt. 5:6).

"Why are we Christians so poverty stricken?" asked A. W. Tozer. "I think it is because we have not learned that God's gifts are meted out according to the taker, not according to the Giver. Though almighty and all wise, God yet cannot pour a great gift into a small receptacle." Tozer then elaborated on five things that are necessary to receive in a measure more in keeping with God's liberality: faith, capacity, receptivity, responsibility, and gratitude.[1]

The gifts once received, similarly never operate automatically, for man is responsible for his use of them. Timothy could either neglect or *stir up* the gift that was in him (1 Tim. 4:14; 2 Tim. 1:6). Certainly Paul would not consider it spiritual if anyone said, "If God wants me to have a gift, He will give it without my interference," or "If God wants the gift stirred up in me, He will have to do the stirring." No. Paul's attitude becomes divine command. *We* are responsible for using the gifts God grants. And Peter adds his "Amen" (1 Pet. 4:10-11).

Casualness or indifference have never been Christian virtues. God gives as He will (1 Cor. 12:11), but while all good gifts come down to us from the Father (James 1:17), they do not come without prayer. It is our task to receive them and to exercise them responsibly. Thus we are told to "earnestly desire the higher gifts," to "earnestly desire the spiritual gifts," to "earnestly desire to prophesy," and also to pray for specific gifts in addition to those already possessed (1 Cor. 14:13).

Those who are "waiting for God" should see that He is frequently waiting for them. Many do not have because they do not ask. Or they may be asking from wrong motives, or without checking on the will of God (James 4:2-3).

(c) A further reason for seeking spiritual gifts is that *each believer has the responsibility and privilege of benefiting others* by rightly exercising any ministry gift he has received (1 Cor. 12:11). We should desire that the lost should be saved, others enriched and the church built up (1 Cor. 12:7; 14:12). When someone in the congregation requires healing, conviction, discernment of spirits, edification, comfort, etc., every Christian should pray that any deficiency will be met fully. Where gifts will help, each should pray that they will be given, for no natural resources of personality, or knowledge of modern counselling technique, can adequately satisfy deep spiritual and emotional needs. But the Christian has access to his Friend above all friends, and can say, "Father, a friend of mine has arrived and I have nothing within myself to set before him. I am dependent upon you. If his need is to be supplied, you will first have to give me the spiritual food that will best provide for his condition" (see Luke 11:5-10).

This compassion and love for others will motivate us to appropriate and apply God's prescription in the most practical and Christ-glorifying way. We desire to become recipients that we might become donors (John 7:37-38); not that we may keep, but that we may bestow; not that we may retain or store up private blessings for ourselves, but because gifts from the Spirit, the Holy One, have power to exalt the unseen and eternal God and bring men face to face with His living reality.

We live today where Satan and the forces of darkness are exerting their devilish power, and are receiving glory from their subjects. Every Christian should therefore earnestly desire gifts that will demonstrate, as in the early Church, that Christ's touch still has undiminished power.

Some are reluctant to desire spiritual gifts lest they take priority over desiring Jesus himself. But gifts and Giver do not vie for position (Matt. 6:11; 7:11; Luke 12:32; 1 Cor. 12:31; 14:1; Eph. 1:17). Certainly the Giver will be sought first, but there is no more conflict between gifts and Giver than between salvation and the Savior, or between the fruit of the Spirit and the Spirit himself. It is quite valid to seek first God's kingdom and His righteousness— not only God himself (Matt. 6:33), for Jesus would not otherwise have commanded it.

If we restrict our seeking to less than God invites us to do, it is not true spirituality but false. We do not honor Him by ignoring or modifying His invitations.

To sum up then: it is obviously not wrong to pray for, and be open to, gifts to use for God. Neither is it wrong to pray that the gifts when imparted will always be exercised prayerfully, responsibly, lovingly, for God's glory and the building up of people. If there is any lack in God's Church or among individuals, the very attitudes of trust, prayer, love, submissiveness, and openness to

Him will place us in a position where those gifts can most readily be granted.

"The fear of counterfeit if we seek gifts"

There is a counterfeit of every gift, and, contrary to what many believe, of every fruit of the Spirit as well. People can believe they have a true expression of gifts or fruit when it is not the genuine article.

Behind all rebellion shown against the Lord there is "the spirit that is now at work among the children of disobedience" (Eph. 2:2). This spirit manifested itself by bringing hardness of heart, unbelief, or in plotting against Jesus and the truth (John 8:39-44; 13:2; 1 John 3:8). On other occasions when Jesus walked among the people, an evil spirit would sometimes be stirred up and would cry out or scream, or convulse a person terribly (Mark 1:23-26; 9:25-26; Luke 4:33-35). Yet Jesus was not responsible for the demons being in the man. Instead, His holy presence had caused the evil spirits already there to be disturbed and to express their evil personalities. Until then, their dangerous work went largely undetected (see also Acts 8:6-7).

Similarly today, a demonic spirit may be present in a person before he becomes a Christian, or sometimes even enter afterwards, where a walk of holiness and submission has been neglected. In such cases, when the anointing power of the Lord comes upon that already inhabited life, there can sometimes be a display of the evil presence. Therefore it is possible to pray for people, and on rare occasions find that a demonic spirit is stirred up, which then blasphemes God in some known language. Praying did not bring it there: praying made it so uncomfortable and agitated that the facade came off, and Satan's earlier undercover activity stood revealed. But God has provided for these situations by making available to us the gift of discerning of spirits which can give immediate recognition that the language source is not divine but demonic. Then the evil force may be expelled by the power of God, either immediately, or later in a private counselling situation. Once deliverance is accomplished, the way is open to receive the Spirit's fullness and an entirely new and beautiful language given by Him.

Some who have heard of these demonic manifestations wrongly place *all* or most tongues in this category. Others, influenced by the false teaching that the gifts are not for today, are completely closed to the suggestion that any current manifestation of tongues can be a genuine and beneficial gift of God. Colored by their own error, they have no alternative but to find fault and hold in contempt or fear that which really is pure and honoring to God. In these cases the traditions of men have replaced the commandments of God.

Many sincere Christians have often been discouraged from seeking all God has for them because they fear they could open themselves to counterfeit manifestations, and Satan might capitalize on their seeking. Yet the early Christians showed no such hesitation, although they were more aware than we are of the countering work of the world, the flesh and the devil. They knew what Jesus had said regarding the willingness of their heavenly Father to give the Holy Spirit and spiritual gifts to those who ask Him. They knew too that Peter and John went to the believers in Samaria and prayed that they would receive the Holy Spirit, without any suggestion of an evil spirit being received or permitted access to their surrendered hearts. The reason is surely obvious: if a person sincerely and honestly approaches the Lord in prayer, there is no possible danger of Him giving the devil's counterfeit. Jesus makes it clear that if the Father did not keep His word, He would be worse than an evil man, for even an evil man knows how to give good gifts to his children (Luke 11:9-13).

If we ask *our Father* for a greater sense of Christ's reality in our lives, and ask Him for the ability to pray in the Spirit and have other gifts that we can exercise in our ministry for Him, He will not give us some counterfeit serpent which will turn around to bite or poison us. Our heavenly Father can be trusted in this area as in all others. He cannot deny himself or His own Word. We can rest in the confidence that if we ask for grace or a grace-gift from the God of all grace, He cannot respond by giving a satanic counterfeit, any more than He could deceive or deny a sincere seeker who comes to Him for salvation. God remains trustworthy. And should a previously undetected oppressing spirit be discovered, that too is progress! Then Christ's power is present to be invoked in delivering the sincere seeker, for He came to "proclaim liberty to the captives, and the opening of the prison to those who are bound" (Isa. 61:1; Luke 4:18).

12

Must All Tongues Be Interpreted?

Some who do not speak in tongues insist that those who do must always have it interpreted. But this is a judgment based on a misunderstanding.

We saw earlier that the Bible reveals two distinct practices concerning tongues. In one case, the rules are *"only two or three, only one at a time, and only with interpretation"* (see 1 Cor. 14:27). The other shows *all praying in tongues, all together, with no interpretation!* (see Acts 2:4; 10:44-46; 19:1-7). The explanation is found in the distinction between the authoritative utterance given before the gathered church, and the act of personal prayer and praise which may be made in a corporate setting or during private devotions (e.g., 1 Cor. 14:18, 28).

When the gift of tongues is spoken or sung in a solo public utterance it always requires interpretation, but when spoken or sung in personal communion with the Lord this further gift is unnecessary.

1. Had interpretation been necessary after personal prayer and praise in tongues we would expect it to be clearly stated. Paul did not say, for example: "I thank God I speak in tongues *and interpret* so that I can understand the content of each phrase." Neither did he say: "I want you all to speak in tongues *and interpret.*" The person who speaks in tongues, without any second gift of interpretation, "speaks to God" and "utters mysteries in the Spirit" (1 Cor. 14:2-3). A believer builds himself up on his most holy faith" simply by praying in tongues (see 14:4; Jude 20).

2. There is no record of interpretation being prayed for, expected, required or experienced after the tongues at Jerusalem, Caesarea or Ephesus (see Acts 2; 10; 19). In such important and detailed narratives, interpretation would not have been passed over in silence if it had in fact occurred. Even in Acts 2 where the *hearers* understood what was said, the 120 Christians did not know the

meaning of each phrase they uttered—for example, those who knew no Cappadocian or Phrygian dialects, yet were speaking in those languages! Neither is there any evidence that the listeners from the many language groups gave the interpretation back to the 120, or that the 120 ever found out the detailed content of their own tongue.

3. Speaking in tongues by itself and without interpretation is listed in 1 Cor. 12 as *one complete gift*, not half a gift, which testifies to it having a purpose complete in itself in some area of spiritual life.

4. Interpretation is required only when it has a purpose *outside* the individual speaker—only when others such as the "other man," or "the church" are involved (see 14:5, 12-19). In other words, when others have been involved through a public utterance, he who speaks in tongues should pray for the power to interpret its content.

5. In the congregation, a person can continue to speak in tongues softly or in the privacy of his own heart (1 Cor. 14:28). It still retains its validity and value, but it is limited to personal communion rather than a public gift offered to the Body.

6. In private praying in tongues we know the general area of our prayer without the need for a further gift of interpretation. We know we are having communion with the Lord. More specifically, we know whether we are praising, adoring, giving thanks, interceding, agonizing, or expressing heart hunger for more of God. (In intercession, for example, the person and situation may be known, but not the full content of the prayer.) Thus tongues must not be considered as being exercised in some mental vacuum or with no knowledge of overall content! There is no exact verbal equivalent for a heartfelt handshake with someone bereaved, or the tenderness of parents with their dangerously ill child, or the touch of two people who love each other, yet communication is effected and acknowledged in the spirit. In the same way, Christians can know the general direction of this communication with the Lord without understanding the exact meaning of individual words spoken. But though this is known within the spirit, and the testimony of the Holy Spirit underlines its authenticity, it is not the same as interpretation.

In experience, the Spirit also bears witness with our spirit that we are being built up in our relationship with the Lord and in faith and sensitivity to Him when we continue to pray in tongues. This inner witness may include an awareness in our spirit of refreshing, peace or repose in God, or some other positive blessing.

Earlier it was mentioned that personal communion with the Lord can take place in a setting of public worship, for worship is not primarily a mass function but the response of an individual to his God. When a group chooses to unite in worshipping Him in tongues, their individual praises may *blend* into a group response, but every expression comes from a separate individual. Interpretation is, therefore, not required (see Acts 2:4-12; 10:44-47; 19:1-7). If the Christians are sensitive to the Spirit and to those around them, unbelievers who are seeking the Lord realize that He is there and is being worshipped by those who love Him.

13

The Nature of Interpretation of Tongues

Are we to understand interpretation of tongues as the interpretation of the *prayer* in tongues, or can it be *God's response* to that prayer?

Not a Message to Men

Some believe that the public utterance of tongues and their interpretation may not simply be in prayer form, but be a message from God to men. We will consider various suggestions for this before turning to a more satisfying explanation.

1. *"The writing on the wall and its inspired interpretation by Daniel expressed in type that tongues and interpretation can sometimes be from God toward men (see Dan. 5:5-28)."*

But this must be rejected, for there is no resemblance between a hand writing *independently of man* upon a wall, and a Christian speaking in tongues when indwelt by the Spirit and co-operating with God. It is best understood as some isolated code or symbolic words written to arrest and disturb, and to show that above men's arrogance and rebellion, God has the final say.

2. *"First Corinthians 14:21 with its connection with Isaiah 28:11-12 supports tongues as messages to men."*

But these texts are insufficient, for in the original reference, the tongues spoken were by foreign invaders, not by the people of God at all, and they were the *naturally* acquired languages of their birth. There is no parallel *at this point* with the gift of tongues. (For the reason Paul introduced Isa. 28:11 to his discussion on tongues, see the commentary on 1 Cor. 14:21-22 in the author's book, *Love and Gifts.*)

3. *"Tongues and interpretation may be a message to the con-*

102

gregation, because both gifts together equal prophecy. And as prophecy is directed to man, tongues and interpretation will flow in that same direction."

But when Paul writes: "He who prophesies is greater than he who speaks in tongues, unless someone interprets . . ." (1 Cor. 14:5), he is not affirming that interpreted tongues *equal* prophecy but that it has *equal value* with prophecy. Two articles may be identical in value, and yet be totally different things. A suit of clothes is equal in value to the money paid over for its purchase, but suit and money bear no resemblance to each other, though their material worth is equal.

4. *"Interpretation may be in the form of revelation, knowledge, prophecy or teaching, on the basis of 1 Cor. 14:6."*

This is unlikely because had Paul meant to refer to interpretation it could reasonably be expected that he would have used that word as in verse 5. The construction of 14:6 is recognized as being very condensed, but its sense is clear. Paul is saying: "Now, brethren, I've just stated that after public utterance in tongues, interpretation is imperative. If, contrary to my usual custom, I come to you solely speaking in tongues, how shall I benefit you? I will not do so at all unless I address myself to your conscious minds and bring you some revelation (either of the meaning of the prayer in tongues or revelation in general), or knowledge or prophecy or teaching."

5. *"Experience confirms these arguments. We believe that our existing practice is permissible because God blesses it and we know intuitively it is right."*

In some circles, in spite of verses to the contrary, most interpreted tongues are regarded as messages to the congregation. But intuition or experience are unreliable guides. Only when Scripture decides the issue for us can we have greater scope to grow into the fullness of God's provision for His Body. Only when we ourselves take the Bible as our rule of faith and practice on these doctrines can we expect to be heard on others (see Matt. 7:3-5). Then the whole Church is strengthened in the truth.

Always Interprets the Prayer

Interpretation of tongues always interprets the prayer so that others can identify with the expression of worship or prayer offered to the Lord. Because of the interrelationship between tongues and their interpretation, both gifts have to be considered when assessing the nature of interpretation.

1. Speaking in tongues is categorically stated to be *directed not to men* (1 Cor. 14:2). It is not a 'message' in which God speaks to us, for if He wants to do that, He speaks through prophecy (1 Cor. 14:3).

2. Whether in public or private worship, speaking in tongues is *always addressed to God*. This is emphasized in various ways. The believer is said to speak to God, pray, pray with the spirit, sing with the spirit, bless the Lord, and give thanks (see 1 Cor. 14:2, 13-17). That interpretation is in the form of prayer is also spelled out, for thanksgiving in a tongue is interpreted *as thanksgiving*. As a result the congregation can add their "Amen" of agreement.

When Paul says, "But if there is no one to interpret, let each of them keep silence in church and speak to himself and to God" (1 Cor. 14:28), he shows there are only two alternatives: *to speak to God publicly* and have it interpreted, or, if no interpreter is present, *to speak to God privately*. Paul is saying, "Under God's anointing, speak to Him publicly in your worship and wait for the interpretation. However, if there is no interpreter present, continue to speak in tongues to God, but do so privately." In both cases the tongue is directed to God.

3. When the 120 spoke in tongues at Pentecost, as with those at Caesarea, *they were speaking to God* and obviously praising Him for His mighty acts of salvation in Christ. At Pentecost there was no interpretation because the hearers could already understand. Yet what they understood was *not God's response* to the tongue in the form of exhortation, encouragement or consolation, but a continuation of the praise and worship which had been offered before any spectators arrived. God was being exalted and extolled by the tongues of His Spirit-filled people.

4. "Interpretation of *tongues*" is nothing more nor less than *the interpretation of the tongues utterance just given*.[1] It will not change the content or reverse the direction of the prayer, for if it did, it would still leave the original tongue uninterpreted, and earn Paul's and the Lord's displeasure.

Some depth of meaning is unavoidably lost in any word-for-word translation, as, for example, in a literal translation of *The Lamb of God*, *agapē*, *Paraklētos*, or *Logos* in the prologue of John's Gospel. These have meanings and associations not readily conveyed in English. This will also happen with tongues, for the language of the Spirit extends beyond the limitations of the human mind. Yet while the tongues-speaker retains within himself some depth of meaning and blessing that cannot be fully conveyed by interpretation, much of its meaning and mood can be expressed in this way.

5. Because interpreted tongues expresses Spirit-inspired adoration or prayer, *it fills a spiritual gap in our worship*. If instead of this, the direction of the utterances had been manward, it would *duplicate* the purpose of prophecy and contribute nothing that prophecy cannot do. But God does not duplicate the function of any of these gifts, especially when in doing so a unique expression of tongues would remain uninterpreted.

When a Christian who is sensitive to the inspiration and mood of the Spirit brings an anointed tongues utterance, his contribution adds to the depth of the public worship. If, for example, adoration is being brought in the language of the Spirit, the utterance will be characterized by beauty and reverence, and we become aware that we are standing on holy ground. And with the interpretation there is opportunity to identify further with worship which has a supernaturally attractive quality, and which edifies the congregation. Sadly, it would be unrealistic to infer that all tongues and interpretation today are of this quality. Nevertheless, this is God's intention, and we should be satisfied with nothing less.

The Indwelling Spirit Praying

The nearest approach we get to tongues having *instructive* value for the congregation is in Rom. 8:26-27, but even here the word 'message' is a misnomer. Here we have the hallowed thought that the Spirit himself intercedes through us, expressing a profound burden of inspired prayer to the Father.

God the Spirit is described as praying from within our human spirit. When the yearnings and sighs take the form of tongues and are then interpreted, we become aware of the very heartbeat of the Spirit. The veil is drawn aside, and we overhear and share His mind and deep desire. We stand upon holy ground, for God is revealing himself. Having overheard such a supernatural burden expressed to the Father, we cannot remain the same. The prayer has become an illustration to us of God's holy love and desire for us and the world, and an expression of that love. (In a similar way, the High Priestly prayer of Jesus, recorded in John 17, becomes instructive.) If we in the congregation truly desire a deeper walk with God, the prayer has a purifying and deeply humbling effect, and draws our response of awe, adoration, and deep dedication.

The *emphases* within our praying in tongues can, of course, change. Usually the emphasis is on *our* praying by the Spirit's enabling, but at times we are aware that *the indwelling Spirit himself* is even more prominent, and is praying through us in the way outlined above. Yet in either case, interpretation will cause others to identify with the prayer, and make their own response to it.

While maintaining the prayer content of tongues, God in His sovereignty may occasionally inspire tongues with an *extended* purpose, though not a contrary purpose. For example, at Pentecost, speaking in tongues was prayer, but in addition it was a vindication of Jesus and a unique expression of God's desire and ability to be known among peoples of all tongues. (See chapter five.)

Although the Bible affirms the gift of tongues is directed not to men but to God, this is not to deny that God can suddenly and miraculously impart the gift of speaking foreign languages/tongues *for evangelistic or similar purposes.* In such cases the utterance is immediately understood and therefore requires no interpretation, and the direction is, of course, obviously from God to men. However, such a wonderful and instantaneous enabling is, as has been expressed elsewhere, not the gift Paul has in mind when he discusses tongues either with or without interpretation: it is better classified as *the working of a miracle* in the realm of language; it is not an example of speaking in tongues which Paul confines to the area of prayer. A parallel to this is seen in the healing ministry; a popular interpretation which has much to commend it, is that divine healings which take place progressively are the result of the gift of healing, while instantaneous healings are better understood as the gift of the working of a miracle in the realm of healing. In both cases definite healings occur, but a different gift operates in each instance.

Wait for Interpretation

What do we say to the fact that godly Christians have from time to time brought a gift which they believed was interpretation, since it followed tongues? We stand in great debt to saintly people who have responded to God in the best way they knew. They, with us, are all learning in this time of restoration. It seems probable, however, that some have been more affected by pentecostal tradition than they realized, and assumed their interpretation would be along the line of exhortation, encouragement and consolation. As a result they dismissed the prompting of the Spirit in the form of interpretation of prayer or praise in tongues. Also, because the Spirit's anointing came upon them after the tongue, they mistook for interpretation what was really a prophecy. If, however, the congregation had continued to wait on God for the interpretation, this also would have been received.

Thus, after a tongues utterance there should be a time of waiting upon God so that the content and mood of the Spirit-inspired prayer can be expressed through interpretation. Only after that should any prophecy be brought. It will have become richer by waiting on God's timing.

Sometimes the one who brings the interpretation of tongues expressing praise or prayer will be inspired to continue straight into prophecy, which may, of course, be God's response to the prayer. In this case *two* gifts are manifested in succession: the prayer in tongues is interpreted, and then prophecy follows.

If prophecy is brought immediately after tongues, there is obvious need for educating and encouraging the congregation to pray for the interpretation. By doing this, the church will conform more closely to divine order, become more sensitive to the Lord's voice, express more variety in the manifestations and bring greater glory to Him.

Nothing is lost, but a further dimension is gained.[3]

14

Is Prophecy the Same as Preaching?

It is common in some traditions to assume that present-day preaching is equivalent to New Testament prophecy. People with these views believe that when they preach they minister in the highest gift, and that to "earnestly desire to prophesy" is to long to preach and teach God's Word. They often define prophecy very broadly as "the proclamation of God's message."

Yet such a vague all-encompassing definition glosses over clear-cut scriptural distinctions.

Not the Same

The following considerations demonstrate that preaching or teaching are not the same as prophecy.

1. *The word "prophecy" is quite different and not interchangeable.* The words for "to preach the gospel" (*euangelizō*), "to preach or proclaim" (*kērussō*), or "to teach" (*didaskō*) are entirely different from the word rendered "to prophesy" (*prophēteuō*). As stated when we considered 1 Cor. 12:10 in *Love and Gifts*, this latter word means "to speak before; to stand in front of God as His mouthpiece and pass on His message." It refers to speaking forth while standing before God as His "go-between," and giving His message as it is received. We find this thought amplified in Deuteronomy: "I will raise up for them a prophet . . . and I will put my words in his mouth, and he shall speak to them all that I command him" (Deut. 18:18).

The Bible never confuses its terms by referring to prophecy as "prophecy" in one place and "preaching or teaching" in another. In 1 Corinthians where prophecy is discussed in detail, there is not the slightest indication of an interchange of words.

2. *Prophets in the Church were not the same as preachers of the Word.* The Bible distinguishes between their ministries. Some are "prophets, some evangelists, some pastors and teach-

ers" (Eph. 4:11). Prophets, here, are not evangelistic preachers, teachers of the Word, or pastors, but have a category of their own. These prophets were men who spoke in the churches under the direct prompting of the Holy Spirit (Acts 11:27-28; 13:1-2; Mark 11:32; John 4:19; 1 Cor. 12:28; 1 Pet. 1:10-12).

3. *"The gift of prophecy" likewise never refers to preaching or teaching the Word*—either in the Gospels (Matt. 26:67-68; Luke 1:67; John 11:51), in Acts (2:16-18; 3:18-21), in the Epistles (1 Thess. 5:19-21; 1 Tim. 1:18; 4:14; 2 Pet. 1:21; 2:1), or in Revelation (10:11). Those who prophesied spoke truths that they could not possibly know solely by study and prayer, but which required a special unveiling of a portion of God's knowledge and purposes. It is clear that "preaching to others" or "teaching" cannot be substituted for the word "prophesying" in any of these or other references.

4. *Unlike preaching, prophecy is in proportion to our faith (Rom. 12:6-8).* It is this faith which opens the door to direct revelation, whereas preaching is more directly related to meditation and study of the Word of God, and the application of scriptural truth to meet people's needs.

If teaching was the same as prophesying Paul would not have included prophecy in a separate category of ministries in Romans 12.

5. *Unlike preaching, prophecy has its source in sudden revelation.* In the exercise of prophecy the utterance arises from the impulse of a sudden revelation or inspiration rather than from a prepared discourse. The idea of speaking from a new and immediate discovery is clear from the use of the Greek word *apokalypsis* in the context of 1 Cor. 14:29-30. God is the author of the words which He conveys to the prophet, and through him to the people. The message comes as a donation of words to the one God is using to prophesy. Peter stated the same truth when he wrote: "No prophecy ever came by the impulse of man, but men moved by the Holy Spirit spoke from God" (2 Pet. 1:21).

Obviously someone known as a prophet can serve in other ways, such as teaching or preaching (Acts 15:32), just as he can be used by God in prayer, in liberality, in giving aid and in acts of mercy (Rom. 12:6-10). A person is not confined solely and forever to one task. Sometimes there may be an interweaving of preaching, prophesying and praying, so that one leads directly into the other. For example, on the Day of Pentecost when Peter preached under the Spirit's anointing, his message contained many prophetic utterances and new facets of truth which he could not then have declared with such confidence without the Spirit's inspiration (Acts 2:14-36). No exegesis of any text could supply him with that knowledge. It had to come through revelation. The prophetic element is only possible as the result of the direct revealing of the Spirit of God.

Some have supposed that preaching and prophesying must be the same because they both can edify, exhort and comfort (1 Cor. 14:3). However, vastly different aspects such as scripture reading, teaching, the word of knowledge and the Lord's Supper also minister edification, exhortation and comfort. So while the gift of prophecy edifies, it is illogical to conclude that everything which edifies must be prophecy.

What Then Is Prophecy?

Many scholars draw attention to the directness and instantaneous nature of prophecy. We note three of them.

M. R. Vincent has written that prophecy is "utterance under immediate inspiration: delivering inspired exhortations, instructions or warnings. The fact of direct inspiration, distinguished prophecy from 'teaching'. . . . The essence of the prophetic character is immediate intercourse with God."[1]

Referring to prophecy in 1 Cor. 14:29-30, C. K. Barrett comments: "It is supernaturally inspired speech and not prepared sermons that is in question," while on Rom. 12:6 he writes: "Prophecy . . . was an immediate communication of God's Word to His people, through human lips and in intelligible speech."[2]

F. F. Bruce expresses similar views when he writes: "The gift of prophecy in the apostolic Church was like the gift of tongues in that it was exercised under the immediate inspiration of God; it differed from it in that it was expressed in the speaker's ordinary language."[3]

Where there are clear lines of distinction in God's Word, they must not be obliterated. A heavy price is paid for vagueness when the scriptures are specific. The failure to define clearly the true nature of prophecy and its connection with inspired revelation creates a vacuum which leads straight to prejudice, confusion, imbalance and false teaching. The view that preaching is the equivalent of prophesying can only be maintained in defiance of New Testament teaching. It is clearly a human accommodation to our unbelief and traditions. It effectively reduces and confines God's power to communicate with men. Because of this error within evangelicalism there has developed a suspicion of anything which is not derived from intellectual study and understanding of God's Word, and this has robbed us of a legitimate source of directly flowing inspiration.

But to say that prophecy is not preaching or teaching is not to say it is superior or inferior to either: it is simply *different*. Preaching and teaching are essential for growth and full development into maturity. As we are all to be witnesses to Jesus, with the responsibility to proclaim Him in word and deed, we all need to study the Word conscientiously. However, preaching and teaching do lack the direct revelation and divine authority which Scripture reveals are the distinguishing marks of a prophetic utterance. It must not be forgotten that teachers and preachers are not above the apostolic directive to "earnestly desire spiritual gifts," and prophecy in particular. Their teaching is not in place of other spiritual gifts, but is complemented by any such additional gifts that God may express through them (see 1 Tim. 4:13-14; 2 Tim. 1:6).

The Difference Illustrated

Melito of Sardis was a distinguished Christian teacher and apologist from the second century, but his ministry was by no means confined to teaching. Among some recently discovered papyri there is the record of him preaching when he suddenly breaks into prophecy and Christ speaks through him directly. The vast difference between preaching/teaching and prophesying is immediately obvious. We break in to Melito's preached message just before he begins to prophesy:

. . . The Lord, having put on human nature, and having suffered for him who suffered, having been bound for him who was bound, and having been buried for him who was buried (in sin) is risen from the dead, and loudly proclaims this message:
Who will contend against me? Let him stand before me.
It is I who delivered the condemned. It is I who gave life to the dead.
It is I who raised up the buried. Who will argue with me?
It is I, says Christ, who destroyed death. It is I who triumphed over the enemy,
And trod down hades, and bound the strong man,
And snatched mankind up to the heights of heaven. It is I, says Christ.
So then, come here all you families of men, weighed down by your sins

And receive pardon for your misdeeds. For I am your pardon.
I am the Passover which brings salvation. I am your life, your resurrection.
I am your light, I am your salvation, I am your King.
It is I who bring you up to the heights of heaven.
It is I who give you the resurrection there.
I will show you the eternal Father. I will raise you up with my own right hand. [4]

In this passage we see how Melito became aware even while he was preaching that the Lord was about to bring a prophetic utterance through him, a message which could not help greatly enriching his hearers.

To *all* Christians (see 1 Cor. 1:2), Paul commands: "Make love your aim, and earnestly desire the spiritual gifts, *especially that you may prophesy*" (1 Cor. 14:1).

15

The Vocal Ministry of Women in the Church

New Testament Evidence in General

Early in the gospel story when the godly prophetess Anna was in the temple, the Lord inspired her to speak of the Messiah to the other worshippers (see Luke 2:36-38).

Throughout His earthly ministry, Jesus welcomed the ministry of women. He accepted the public testimony of the Samaritan woman, who in her amazement and joy then preached to a whole city. And God honored this spontaneous witness and used it to draw many men to Jesus where they could hear His words for themselves (see John 4:28-42).

Mary was chosen to share the news of the empty tomb with the disciples when the Lord could have given this honor to a man (John 20:1-2). Soon after, she became the very first to see the risen Lord, and was also the privileged one commissioned to carry His world-shattering resurrection message to the believers gathered together in His name (John 20:14-18).

Men and women repeatedly prayed together (Acts 1:14-15). Soon afterwards when the Spirit descended, both were heard worshipping together in tongues. Both took part in the Lord's Supper, prayer and praise (Acts 2:4, 42-47).

Male and female were blessed with the same inheritance in Christ (see Gal. 3:28). Both were of equal worth.

Joel had promised that there would be daughters and maidservants among those who prophesied when the Spirit was poured out, and Peter reminded the crowd of this when they gathered in amazement on the Day of Pentecost (Joel 2:28-29; Acts 2:17-18). Later in Acts, Priscilla assisted her husband Aquila in instructing Apollos in doctrine (Acts 18:24-26), and there is no suggestion that this was improper. Paul wanted everyone to prophesy (1 Cor. 14:5, 24, 31), and neither he nor Philip attempted to curb

Philip's four daughters who did so with sufficient regularity to earn its mention by Luke (Acts 21:7-9). Men were not given a monopoly of the Spirit's gifts for use in public ministry or corporate worship.

It is clear therefore, that Joel, our Lord, Peter, the assembled men of the early Church, Aquila, Philip and Paul, and Luke who records these occasions, in no way minimize the ministry of women to mixed gatherings of the Lord's people.

The Bible knows nothing of meetings solely open to Christian women who can pray, praise, exercise gifts and judge the utterances. Both men and women could minister in these ways as long as they were suitably attired, submissive to God's appointed order, and willing to have their revelation judged (see 1 Cor. 11:4-5; 14:29-32).

Paul's Instruction to Corinth

Every member without distinction of sex is gifted for ministry (12:7-11), and each may participate in the fellowship (e.g., 14:26). It is not just 50 percent of the Christian population which has a particular function to fulfill, for all within the Body, whether male or female, have this responsibility. Without the ministry of both, the church will not function properly (12:12-27). Paul wants everyone to take part (14:5, 24, 31). Consequently, when he enjoins silence upon the women in 1 Cor. 14:33-35, he is not commanding unqualified silence during congregational singing, praise, prayer or prophecy. Both sons and daughters did all these things in public ministry and were completely within the divine will. It would contradict New Testament precedents and Paul's earlier instructions if women could neither pray nor prophesy in public worship (see 11:4-13).

Jewish influence was considerable in and around Corinth (see Acts 18). The Jewish leaders, like the Greeks, regarded a woman's ability to appreciate and understand truth as minimal, and others soon reflected their attitude. Opportunities of education for women were almost nonexistent. One rabbinic saying stated that to teach a woman the law was "to cast pearls before pigs." It was believed that just as pigs could not appreciate pearls, neither could women appreciate the value of the truths they heard nor comment intelligently upon them. Thus in an age when customs and understanding were so different from our own, education for women was overlooked, ·and their ability to contribute intelligently restricted. Consequently many grew lax and undisciplined. But with conversion to Christ vast changes in their standing occurred. Life became more meaningful, for now they were reverenced and honored within the Christian community as 'sisters' with a soul of their own. Yet another problem quickly arose, for they had difficulty adjusting to their new-found freedom, and their lack of discipline now expressed itself during worship. It seems likely that they had begun interrupting and disturbing the services with simple or ill-timed questions. Or some may have been commenting 'knowingly' among themselves as the teaching was being given.

Paul, however, would not have these women in any way distracting or controlling the meeting with their questions and comments. He honored their status but would not permit any disorder to hinder the deeper presentation of truth. Any inappropriate questions would be better answered at home where they would present the men with the wholesome challenge of ministering first to their own households. By forbidding any undisciplined interruptions, worship and teaching could flow in unity without cross currents, and peace and order be maintained. Immodest dress or unedifying behavior in general was also forbidden. Nothing that would bring upon the young Church the faintest suspicion of feminine immodesty or carelessness of speech could remain unchecked. Women were honored among Christians more than anywhere else in the world, but they had to understand the limitations of this privilege. They could not assume the role of teachers in public worship, or "lord it over (*authenteō*) men" (see 1 Tim. 2:11-12; 1 Cor. 14:34).

When people led others in an expression of adoration and intercession, they became, for that moment, *the mouthpiece of the gathered church*. They submerged their individual identity and represented the group when they said, "*We* praise you. . . . *We* pray." Similarly, men or women who brought a public utterance in tongues and interpretation became the inspired spokesmen of the congregation, while the congregation expressed its participation with an "Amen" of agreement (see 14:16).

In contrast, when a Christian prophesied, he or she became *the mouthpiece of God*, and represented God's voice to the congregation. Therefore, when women took part in public prayer or prophesying, their individuality was submerged and they spoke as representatives of the group, or of the Lord. Teaching, however, was in a different category. Although always based on revelation and inspiration, it nevertheless drew instruction from the storehouse of the individual's knowledge of God, His Word, and His ways. The teacher proclaimed the subject God had given, but he stood more as an individual, with individual authority. Therefore if a woman taught in the congregation, her own individuality and authority would take precedence over all in the meeting. Understanding that women are more open to deception if they step into the place of authority, Paul gave specific instructions to avoid this possibility (1 Tim. 2:11-14).

Relevance for Today

Are Paul's commands to the Corinthians to be taken as merely local, or is there an eternal principle here? That there were localized customs and situations in the Bible that called for localized or temporary rulings is not in doubt. For example: In deference to Jewish upbringing and conscience, the Gentiles were to abstain from anything strangled and from blood (Acts 15:20). *The eternal principle*, however, was, "Never put a stumbling-block or hindrance in the way of a brother" (see Rom. 14:13-21; 1 Cor. 8:9-13). Again, in Corinth, the veil that covered the woman's head (not a hat that perches on top of the head!) signified the chaste woman separated to her husband. But Christian women with their new-found liberty in Christ were wanting to be liberated from the custom of being veiled: "All things are lawful: we don't need this headcovering." But Paul countered, "Yes you do, for if you do not wear a veil, you will be identified as an immoral woman, and therefore you will dishonor your husband, and Christ your Lord." *The eternal principle* of avoiding the very appearance of evil necessitated wearing a veil (see 11:4-5, 13; 1 Thess. 5:22), whereas in another society where veiling was not linked with morality, the instruction to be veiled would be meaningless.

In the same way there were some local and temporary rulings in Paul's command to silence, as well as an eternal principle. And even then the command was not absolute, for singing, tongues, interpretation and prophecy by women were still permitted in Corinth and elsewhere.

A woman can serve Christ in many ways, but it is a continuing spiritual principle that no authoritative role over men is permitted (see Eph. 5:21-33; 1 Tim. 2:11-12). This is why positions of spiritual leadership are confined to men. Any woman who will not submit places herself outside the protection of God's appointed order, becomes an immediate target for deception, and brings great confusion to herself and the Church. Edification cannot flow freely when either sex refuses its God-ordained position.

Men will always be far superior to women—at being men; and

women will always be far superior to men—at being women. Each is best in his/her own appointed place. But as Paul is inspired to command a male—even a prophet—to be silent if his continued words were likely to prove unedifying (see 14:30), he could for the same reason command women to refrain from ministering in leadership, or teaching, or making unhelpful remarks during worship.

So the Bible recognizes a woman's place in public prayer and in ministering spiritual gifts. But there was need for caution on teaching, where the individuality of the woman would be conspicuous. The lack of education, prevailing local customs, plus the recognition of man's authority, meant that women were not at liberty to teach men unless they did so under the spiritual covering of husband, father or church leadership (see Acts 18:26; 21:7-9; Heb. 13:17).

Men for their part are to be motivated by nothing less than the example and inspiration of Christ's sacrificial love as they give love and honor to women (see Eph. 5:24-29; 1 Tim. 5:1-2).

Therefore the teaching and spirit of the Scriptures leads us to affirm that in addition to being used in the gifts of the Spirit, there will be occasions when a woman with biblical understanding and insight, and the church's confidence, can teach in the congregation, provided she is submissive and never assumes a position of spiritual oversight (see Acts 18:26). Certainly God has blessed the public ministry of women who have moved under the Spirit's inspiration while submitting to men as their spiritual authority.

So if a woman teaches God's people, her spirit must remain submissive and open to the correction of her own husband and the men in leadership. She must in no way disregard nor usurp their authority, nor seek to take to herself a ministry for which she is neither called nor anointed, and her inspiration must first be recognized and approved by those in leadership. In her submission she finds her protection.

16
Should We Take Doctrine from the Book of Acts?

It is widely taught in some circles that doctrine concerning the Spirit's work should be derived from the didactic or teaching passages of the New Testament, and not from the narrative or historical portions. John R. W. Stott has popularized this view, and at the outset of his study he lays it down as one of his "basic principles of approach." He writes: "What is described in scripture as having happened to others is not necessarily intended for us, whereas what is promised to us we are to appropriate, and what is commanded us we are to obey. . . . I must repeat that a doctrine of the Holy Spirit must not be constructed from purely descriptive passages in the Acts."[1]

Others make similar or even more far-reaching assertions.

It is easy to see that if the above argument is valid, much of Acts and the Gospels must be rejected as source material for doctrine, and the conclusions expressed throughout this book become invalid in so far as they bear upon the Acts material. Conversely, if this argument is invalid and without a solid biblical foundation, any theology built upon it will prove futile and will collapse. So the subject is an extremely crucial one.

It is soon evident, however, that to exclude much of Acts and the Gospels in this way is a tragic and fundamental error with widespread effects. It has misled countless Christians and robbed them of their full inheritance in the Spirit. However well-intentioned this teaching may be, it has a most suffocating effect, and it desupernaturalizes large portions of the Christian gospel for its devotees and those influenced by it.

There are many reasons why this view must be rejected.

1. The testimony of 2 Tim. 3:16-17 is crystal clear: "*All* scripture is inspired by God and profitable for teaching, for reproof, for correction, and for training in righteousness, that the man of God may be complete, equipped for every good work." (*Didaskalia*

[teaching] is also translated "doctrine" in 1 Tim. 1:3; Titus 1:9; 2:10, etc.)

Since the "purely descriptive passages in the Acts" are part of Scripture, they are profitable for teaching right doctrine, reproving false doctrine and correcting inadequate doctrine. It also means that Acts 2, 8, 9, 10 and 19, like other parts of Scripture, are given to make us all righteous, complete, and equipped for serving God and men.

Quite clearly, teaching that there must be no doctrine constructed from "purely descriptive passages" stands in a world apart from the Scriptures themselves. There are simply *no* purely descriptive passages in the Acts.

This evidence alone is conclusive, but there is more.

2. It is illogical and arbitrary to teach that *epistles* addressed to specific congregations in the past reveal God's mind not only for them but for all future generations as well, while the *history* of God's activity within Acts reveals His mind solely for the people who were first involved. Logically, either both are valuable for doctrine, or both must be rejected. *Epistles* written after Pentecost and inspired history enacted after Pentecost express the mind of God for the 20th century. In both we see God working in the lives of others, producing in them what He himself desired. If anyone drives a wedge between biblical theology and biblical experience on any subject, he separates what God has joined together. Apostolic doctrine and action were not at variance but complementary. Christian theology today must reflect the activities of the apostles as well as their teaching, for the apostles guided the Church by inspired example as well as the inspired Word. Any other conclusion is a debilitating tradition of men.

3. Paul's readers were to learn by seeing God's work in others— not just by reading apostolic letters—for Paul wrote: "What you have learned and received and heard and seen in me, do" (Phil. 4:9). One of God's methods of instructing Christians was to teach by visual means so that they observed His activities through inspired participants in specific situations. The believers would not readily forget these lessons. Certainly the many Samaritans, the twelve Ephesians, and Paul himself would not forget that in their own spiritual experience the reception of the Spirit was subsequent to their initial believing.

4. This teaching, even where offered with full explanations,

still relegates these New Testament descriptive passages to secondary importance. As such it comes close to implying that there was only temporary significance in the words and deeds of Jesus and His Spirit found in the narrative sections of the Gospels and in the early Church, while that which the apostles *wrote* retained eternal value. Any such dichotomy must, however, be rejected as entirely foreign to the spirit of the New Testament. It is impossible to believe that the Holy Spirit would record in the Acts only examples of Spirit baptisms which were *not* to be used for future guidance, and, conversely, that He has failed to record any examples which could in fact guide us today.

5. Historical material narrating experience is sometimes found in the *epistles*. First Corinthians 12:13 is a case in point. This verse explains that which had already taken place in the lives of Paul and one specific congregation of believers. It makes no promise that 20th-century Christians would experience the same. Yet it is universally and rightly accepted as having doctrinal application to today. We cannot therefore consistently teach doctrine from historical data in 1 Corinthians yet deny the right to teach it from similar information in Acts.

6. We cannot logically disregard inspired example on the reception of the Holy Spirit within Acts yet teach from its descriptive passages on other doctrines. Acts rightly forms one of the Church's important sources for theology on the resurrection, ascension and glory of Christ (Acts 1, 2, 9, 22, 26), prayer and worship (1, 2, 4, 12, 13), sin and judgment (5, 12), the kingdom of God (8, 14, 19), salvation (2, 3, 8-11, 15, 16), God's various methods of guidance (1-28), the content of New Testament preaching (2, 3, 7, 8, 10, 13, 17), God's ability to empower and heal (2, 3, 4, 8-11, 14, 19, 28), the Church, its organization and officers (1, 6, 15, 20), baptism and the Supper (2, 8-11, 13, 16, 19, 20, 22), missions (1-28), deliverance (8, 16, 19), brotherly love (1, 2), the practical value of the Spirit's gifts (2-28), the Christian life when under attack (5, 7, 8, 9, 13), and so on.

It is noteworthy that theologians do in fact draw doctrinal teaching from the historical and narrative passages within Acts. For example, among the books on my shelves are two well-known and respected major theological works written by different men on the subject of Christian baptism and initiation which between them refer 300 times to passages in Acts. They and other biblical theologians draw heavily on these descriptive passages and rightly derive their doctrine from the entire New Testament.

7. The view that would allow no doctrine from the "purely descriptive passages" in practice also fails to do justice to the doctrinal content of recognized "teaching sections" in the Gospels and epistles as well. In many of these the Holy Spirit's activity is clearly portrayed. Rom. 8:9 is especially significant in this regard, for it has universal application and concerns the Christian doctrine of initiation. (See also Gal. 3:2-5; Eph. 1:13-14; Titus 3:4-6; Luke 11:5-13; Matt. 7:11; Rom. 8:26-27; 12:3-8; 1 Cor. 1:5-7; 12-14; 2 Cor. 3:7-8; Eph. 4:7; 5:18-19; 6:17-18; Phil. 3:3; Col. 3:16; 1 Thess. 1:5-6; 4:8; 5:19-20; Jude 20.)

Some who oppose a "second-experience theology"[2] point out that Acts 8 can be used in favor of a double experience while Acts 10 can support a single experience. We agree! They then claim that this illustrates the danger of arguing from narratives which have no consistency about the them![3] We disagree! The narratives consistently illustrate that God is sovereign, and, in the matter of initiation into the Christian life, He can allow relatively short gaps or no gaps at all, and He can vary the order of events. If we claim there must be two quite separate and distinguishable experiences with an obvious time lapse in between, we are wrong! And if we say they always occur simultaneously, we are again wrong! God has chosen to move in both ways. The consistent testimony of the book of Acts is that whether the initiatory process was short or a little longer, before biblical initiation was complete, participants had heard and personally responded to Christ, been baptized as believers, and had experienced the outpouring of the Spirit in such a way that they and other Christians knew it. The timetable and the order could change but the goal attained was consistently the same.

Quite clearly we are not only to appropriate what Scripture promises and obey what it commands, but also allow ourselves to be arrested and instructed through observing the spiritual destination at which the early Christians arrived. If when we consider the outcome of their life and faith (Heb. 13:7-8) we find that their experience was richer than our own, we have reason to question whether we are on the same theological wave-length!

It is the testimony of the epistles as well as Acts that all Christians everywhere had received the Spirit in an observable way with supernatural evidence. They had a level of experience of the Holy Spirit at the time of their initiation and thereafter to which most Christians today are strangers. If on the matter of salvation our theological position lowered our horizons until we were content with less than New Testament experience, we would have reason to be alarmed. We should, however, be no more content with our experience of the Holy Spirit if it is also less than the early Christians universally experienced.

However we describe it theologically, we should not stop before our salvation, Spirit baptism, fullness, sanctification, everything concerning the richness of our Christian faith, matches that of those in the early Church. Paul could say to a fellow Christian who knew the richness of New Testament experience: "I pray that the *sharing* of your faith may promote the knowledge of all the good that is ours in Christ" (Philem. 6; see Mark 5:19). The same faith that had been delivered to the early Christians was not only to be personally enjoyed, but contended for and imparted to others in all its original content, purity and power (see Jude 3).

Referring to the life of the Church in its early days, James Denny has well said: "Primitive historical Christianity must always be essentially normative, and if later types of religion so diverge from the primitive type as to find the New Testament rather an embarrassment than an inspiration, the question they raise is whether they can any longer be recognized as Christian." [4]

Since the descent of the Spirit at Pentecost, and to this day, the Church has been living in the dispensation of the Holy Spirit (2 Cor. 3:8). The history of the first thirty years of this Age of the Spirit is recorded in the book of Acts. Any current teaching that must minimize this biblical material—written as it was in the same dispensation as we occupy—to justify its theology of the Holy Spirit, at that point advertises its own doctrinal inadequacy and forfeits the right to be called biblical. The Church has tragically suffered as a result of such emasculated teaching at a key point of Christian belief. We gladly acknowledge that God uses Christians with whom we may disagree on various issues, but we cannot sacrifice the Word of God and Christian experience out of courtesy for them.

We can be grateful to God that epistles, history and narrative reinforce and complement each other for the better understanding of biblical doctrine and for the enrichment of the Church. Certainly they all testify to the vivid, definite nature of the Spirit's reception, and to the Christian's experience of Him.

"All scripture is inspired by God and profitable for *didaskalia* (doctrine, teaching), . . . that the man of God may be complete, equipped. . . ." To conclude otherwise is to oppose clear scriptural teaching. It is a house built upon sand.

Preparing to Receive the Holy Spirit

We may readily believe that the early Christians were baptized in the Holy Spirit with the accompanying sign of speaking in tongues, and thereafter manifested other gifts for the blessing of men. And we may have no difficulty accepting that fullness and gifts are for today. But all this is only so much theory unless we are actually experiencing the Lord in this way for ourselves.

This and the following chapter is written to help the seeking Christian experience the fullness of the Spirit in his own life. May I suggest therefore that you first read through both chapters and become acquainted with their overall content, and then re-read them carefully later when you can get aside with the Lord and pray.

It may well be that you have already been well prepared by the Lord for the step of receiving the Spirit. If this is so it could be quite sufficient to give the one instruction: "Receive the Holy Spirit!" and you would immediatedly receive and speak in tongues. Others, however, would find this unhelpful and impractical, so it will be profitable to set out in detail how you can prepare.

The primary obstacle many of us "sophisticated moderns" find to receiving the Holy Spirit with speaking in tongues is not at all our *coming in* to receiving the Spirit with this evidence, but *escaping from* the imprisonment of ignorance, independence, fear, false teaching (for example, that the Spirit is always received at conversion), prejudice, inhibitions, indifference, pride, insincerity, complacency and unbelief. To change the metaphor, we must love God sufficiently to want to come out of "reverse" as the preliminary move to going forward with Him.

It is wonderful if you have never been opposed to speaking in tongues. Sadly, however, many of us at some stage have resisted

God's gift. We may even have fought and taught against it so that when we finally examined the Scriptures and became intellectually convinced that God wanted us to pray in tongues, the negativeness had become such a part of us that our spirits were more deeply affected than we realized. We had developed a resistance to tongues that people in the early Church did not have. They therefore could immediately enter into this pentecostal reality, whereas we had first to come out of religious negativism, and that requires effort and determination (Luke 16:16).

We have found that people who come freshly to the Scriptures concerning baptism in the Spirit and speaking in tongues are able to enter in very naturally and spontaneously, whereas others who have been indoctrinated against tongues are affected by the general unbelief and suspicion and have either consciously or unconsciously shut the door. Before they can proceed they need to open the door to the Lord in a deliberate act of faith.

I am assuming in this chapter that you have already accepted (or are prepared immediately to accept) the Lord Jesus Christ as your own personal Lord and Savior. This is absolutely essential, for you are inviting spiritual confusion if you try to continue a Christian journey that you have not yet started. In other words, you cannot go on with God before you have *started* your life with Him by being born again.

You should also submit to the Lord's command to be baptized (Acts 2:37-38; Matt. 28:16-20). Christian baptism is much more than a commandment, for it is a holy and wonderful privilege granted to every new believer. So much could be said about its value as revealed in Scripture, but that is a subject much too large for us to consider here.

God can of course graciously intervene as He did with Cornelius and baptize you in the Spirit before you are baptized in water. However, if you have not yet taken this step though you claim to belong to Christ, I recommend that you prayerfully obey your Lord and publicly testify in baptism to having turned your back on sin and unbelief and identified yourself with Jesus and His people.

Your expectation and faith will be further released with every step of preparation and obedience, for the Holy Spirit is given to those who *obey* Him (Acts 5:32; see John 14:21).

You do not have to spend weeks trying to receive the Holy Spirit. You could well receive Him very quickly—even in a matter of minutes. The following steps will guide you.

1. *Don't let any particular theological tradition or term stand in your way of receiving what God wants you to have.* If your theology stands in your way of receiving further blessing, you can be sure it is not biblical theology. You need quickly to change it, for it is costing you too much! The pentecostal reality is called by a variety of terms as we saw in the first chapter of this book, so if you are still unsure about the term "baptism in the Spirit" use any of the others! Or simply say: "Lord, I desire you above all else, and I long for the same quality of life in the Spirit that you poured out upon the early Church." Then leave it to the Lord to name it. He'll know what you mean! And He will immediately start to answer the prayer of your heart and guide you as to how to receive.

I now have no doubts that these are valid biblical terms for us to use in prayer, but I didn't always feel this way! It seems foolish now but when I was wanting to receive the enrichment I saw in the early Church, I was still very unsure about whether it was right to pray to be baptized in the Spirit, so I asked the Lord to *fill* me with the Holy Spirit! And although the answer to my prayer for fullness was not immediately *manifest* to the degree it was to become, I accepted God's gift by faith and spoke in tongues. Ten days later when the level of my faith had deepened through responding to the Lord and praying in tongues, I was so immersed and flooded with the very personal Spirit of God that much of my initial hesitation over terms quickly dissolved. If this was not *the* baptism in the Holy Spirit, it could certainly be described as *a* baptism, an immersion in the Spirit and in the love of God! I could now understand better why the Bible and Christians spoke of being *baptized* in the Spirit: it suddenly seemed particularly apt for describing the spiritual reality which had taken place.

We need to be as precise as possible when using biblical words so as not to cause unnecessary offense or hinder others by our carelessness, but I'm convinced that God isn't as interested in our theological niceties as we are. Our theology is helpful only if it leads us and others to God, and this particular aspect of theology does, as hundreds of thousands can gratefully testify.

2. *Remember that the Holy Spirit is Himself a gift to be received.* Neither the Spirit nor His gifts can be earned even by the

very best of human effort. It is only because of God's grace that we can ever experience any aspect of His benevolence. Every good thing that we receive and every ability to respond comes as a gift from His hands. We can fall in line with His purpose only because God is always at work in us to make us willing and able to obey Him (see Phil. 2:13, TEV). Every forward step in the Christian life is possible only because He has taken the initiative and acted in grace.

None of us will therefore ever reach a position where we deserve the blessing of God, regardless of what particular blessing or gift it may be, and regardless of how much we prepare, pray, fast, obey, or do anything else. So if you are trying to be worthy to receive God's gift, forget it, for you will *never* receive that way. The blessing of God is not for sale, but He and His gifts are available free, and available now! The Holy Spirit is none other than "the *gift* of the Holy Spirit" (Acts 2.38; 10:45).

Yet God does not force His undeserved favor upon us. He loves us, offers himself to us, seeks our enrichment; but we are still responsible for the choices we make, and for responding to Him so that we can best receive the gift and gifts of His Spirit.

3. *Be cleansed of all known sin.* On the Day of Pentecost Peter's audience was quickly confronted with the message of the crucified Jesus and was told that they shared responsibility for His death. "What shall we do?" they cried out, as the Holy Spirit convicted them and revealed their sin. And Peter replied: "Repent, and be baptized every one of you . . . and you shall receive the gift of the Holy Spirit" (Acts 2:37-38). [1]

Repentance is an inward change of heart, mind and will, as God enables us to put right any matters which stand between us and Him. Only as sin is confessed and forsaken is a relationship established with the Lord, for if we make light of iniquity the Lord will not listen (Ps. 66:18). We cannot progress into any deeper awareness of Him nor partake of His fullness if there is unconfessed sin, or where restitution is possible but has not been made. Sincerity of heart is measured by a willingness to be changed.

Broken or festering relationships need to be reconciled. A heart filled with resentment, bitterness or pride allows no room for the Spirit of holiness, nor can it be released to offer acceptable spiritual worship and praise. So don't proceed in your search for greater reality in God until these things are dealt with. Leave your offering until you can give it from an undivided heart. Get right with your brother first (Matt. 5:23-24). *Then* come and offer yourself to God.

People who have been involved in the occult or psychic area usually find it much harder to respond to the Lord and be baptized in the Holy Spirit. They find that this is a powerful and dangerous area which binds the human spirit. It puts a man in a spiritual straitjacket so that he cannot move at will.

This isn't surprising, for the Lord has strictly forbidden any investigation or practice in these areas (Deut. 18:9-14), and He never introduces rules without good reason. He knows what is best and what is harmful for us. If He has absolutely forbidden contact with the occult, we can be sure it is because it has the power to bind, drag us down, and destroy. He desires to protect and bless us with His presence and give us liberty, not see us destroyed (Deut. 6:24).

God regards as wickedness such practices as spiritism, fortune-telling, horoscopes, telepathy, hypnotism, divination, cults or false religions; and any involvement with these must be confessed, forsaken, and completely renounced. If your involvement in these practices has been extensive or prolonged, I recommend that you seek counselling help from mature Spirit-filled Christians before asking the Lord to baptize you. All books or objects associated with them should be destroyed to aid in breaking the power of these past experiences (Acts 19:18-19). Only when repentance is sealed with total dissociation can effective prayer be made.[2]

Perhaps you have collected an idol or image as a curio or for ornamental purposes. If so, destroy it—even if a well-meaning missionary gave it to you! This is because representations of other so-called gods or objects of worship or veneration from non-Christian religions are an abomination to the Lord, and must not be given a place of honor (Ex. 20:3-6). Though they may mean little to you, they can be providing an entrance point for the binding power of demonic activity. Only when they are removed and destroyed is the way open for any associated oppression or bondage to be broken.

It was said of the early Christians that they "turned *to* God *from* idols, to serve a living and true God" (1 Thess. 1:9; see 1 Cor. 12:2; Eph. 2:1-5). Repentance always involves a turning from as well as a turning to!

If you have been involved in any of these or similar forbidden areas, here is a prayer you can make your own:

"Father, I now see that any involvement with occult things

is sin and an abomination to you. I now realize your Word speaks strongly against any association with these practices. Father, I am truly sorry for displeasing you in this way and I promise to have nothing more to do with them. I renounce completely all contact with these sinful things, in the name of the Lord Jesus Christ, and I ask you to forgive and cleanse me completely with Jesus' blood. Thank you, Lord, for your wonderful grace. I know you have heard and will answer. I come in the all-conquering name of Jesus. Amen."

4. *Surrender yourself fully to the Lord.* Surrender everything to the Lord that you know stands between you and Him. "I appeal to you therefore, brethren, by the mercies of God, to present your bodies as a living sacrifice, holy and acceptable to God, which is your spiritual worship. Do not be conformed to this world but be transformed by the renewal of your mind, that you may prove what is the will of God, what is good and acceptable and perfect" (Rom. 12:1-2). There is a cost in following Jesus Christ and the Bible never tries to conceal this from us. Some things must go to make room for new loyalties and qualities consistent with Christian commitment.

God is working within us not only to make us more effective witnesses for Him, or to give us spiritual blessings, or to enable us to speak in a new supernatural language, but that we may be holy and like Him. Therefore, while the miracle of receiving the Holy Spirit and speaking in tongues is, from our side, a simple act of faith which is not dependent upon our attaining a certain degree of perfection first, nevertheless there must be a willingness to surrender to Him and to manifest increasingly the fruit of the Spirit.

5. *Understand that faith involves action!* Any forward step in the Christian life involves the exercise of faith, for without faith it is impossible to please God (Heb. 11:6). Faith grows as we respond to God's promises. Yet all too often we are encouraged to exercise faith to receive Christ as Lord and Savior, but then through unbiblical teaching the impression can be left that in that act of conversion we have received everything we require. So we settle down, and instead of using our faith to press on in God we tend to think of it as necessary only to maintain our existing place in Him. Faith seems to go on "stand-by" duty only. Yet exercising saving faith to come to Christ should be

only the beginning of a *life* of faith. For this reason, if some time has elapsed since your conversion, or if you have become an inactive Christian, you may have to relearn some very basic lessons on faith to get yourself moving again!

Throughout Scripture faith is coupled with distinct faith-actions. As God revealed His will to His people they did not examine themselves to see if they had big, little or middle-sized faith. When they knew what God wanted they responded by moving in the direction of His will, and God saw this as faith. Faith was not just something you *had*: it was something you *did* because you trusted the Lord and had been conquered by His love. Faith was translated into action along the direction of the will of God. Quite clearly, the Lord saw openness and obedience and a readiness to advance as faith. It was therefore pleasing to Him and He reckoned it to them as righteousness.

Faith is not just a mental awareness and assent to some particular truth. It *expresses* itself in our obedient response to God's commands and invitations. As such it involves us in doing some very down-to-earth completely human *actions*. Faith without this expression is dead and barren (James 2:17-22).

Many examples in Scripture illustrate this important principle.

God regarded Abel's offering of an acceptable sacrifice as faith. Enoch walked with God and pleased Him, and that was faith. Noah and Abraham obeyed the Lord by taking steps in the direction of the revealed will of God, even to the extent of building a great ark on dry land, or of offering up a son. And God saw their activity as the activity of faith and He reckoned it to them as righteousness (Heb. 11:4-10, 17-19).

Faith, for Moses, meant moving his hand and smiting a rock at the Lord's command. His faith had to get into his hand (Ex. 17:5-6). The children of Israel's faith had to reach their feet, as they moved and stepped into the Red Sea and later the Jordan River (Ex. 14:22; Heb. 11:29; Josh. 3:12-16). There was no trace of a miracle in these actions. The response was completely human, yet when it was made in obedience to God's command the miracle began. It became the "trigger" that activated His power. And for the Israelites, even when they had begun they had to continue to walk to continue the miracle. Their part in it was crucial, but all it required was left, right, left, right, in the direction the Lord wanted them to go!

The Lord had told the Israelites that when they entered the promised land "every place on which your foot treads shall be yours" (Deut. 11:24), but the people had to pick up their feet and move forward in the land under their own human propulsion in order to inherit the promise.

So people suffered abuse, left Egypt, kept the Passover, stepped into the Red Sea, marched around Jericho, welcomed God's people, fought, conquered and refused to bow to evil. These were faith-actions, and they pleased God (Heb. 11:24-37).

Similarly, Elijah in his confrontation with the prophets of Baal not only surrendered himself and his reputation to the Lord, but in an act of faith built an altar, put the offering upon it and called on the Lord. Then when he had done all he could do, his offering was accepted and touched by the fire of God (1 Kings 18:30-38).

Many New Testament passages illustrate this same faith-principle. One woman with a hemorrhage found that the key to her healing was in pressing through the crowd with determination and reaching out and touching Jesus' garment. That was faith in action. Yet such a very ordinary and apparently foolish act released the power of God in her life (Mark 5:25-34).

Faith is not preoccupied with taking its own temperature. Rather, it acts by responding to the Lord's will. Because of this the Bible speaks of "the obedience of faith" (Rom. 1:5, NASB).

It is encouraging that Jesus the Baptizer is described as the Author and Perfecter (Source and Completer) of our faith (Heb. 12:2). He is our Faith-builder, the One to whom we can come when our faith is weak. We can no more increase our own faith than we can lift ourselves up by our own shoelaces, but Jesus can do what we can't do! We can come to Him as another man did whose faith was mixed with a lot of doubt, and say: "I do believe, Lord, but I ask *you* to help my unbelief" (see Mark 9:24).

Come to Him then with the little faith you now have but with a heart that wants to know Him better, and tell Him: "Lord, I know that my faith is very small, and also that without faith it is impossible to please you. Yet I want to please and serve you, Lord, and so I ask you to give me sufficient faith for these next steps of walking with you. Let my halting steps of faith be a love offering that brings you pleasure" (see Luke 17:5).

Don't ask Him for some mighty faith that you can't believe for, but only that which is required for the next few steps of obedience which you need to take. And if you mean it He will give you all you need! Remember, too, that it is not the greatness of our faith that is important, but the greatness of the God in whom we trust. A little faith in a strong bridge will get us to the other side, but great faith in a weak bridge will land us in the river! It's the strength of the bridge, not the faith, that is crucial. We don't trust in our faith, but in the trustworthiness of the Lord.

We will return to the subject of faith a little later.

6. *Re-read the scriptures where the Holy Spirit is promised.* "And it shall come to pass afterward, that I will pour out my spirit [Spirit] on all flesh; your sons and your daughters shall prophesy, your old men shall dream dreams, and your young men shall see visions. Even upon the menservants and maidservants in those days, I will pour out my spirit [Spirit]" (Joel 2:28-29).

"I [John] baptize you with water for repentance, but he who is coming after me is mightier than I, whose sandals I am not worthy to carry; he will baptize you with the Holy Spirit and with fire" (Matt. 3:11; Luke 3:16; Mark 1:8).

"Ask, and it will be given you; seek, and you will find; knock, and it will be opened to you. For every one who asks receives, and he who seeks finds, and to him who knocks it will be opened. What father among you, if his son asks for a fish, will instead of a fish give him a serpent; or if he asks for an egg, will give him a scorpion? If you then, who are evil, know how to give good gifts to your children, how much more will the heavenly Father give the Holy Spirit to those who ask him?" (Luke 11:9-13; Matt. 7:7-11).

"Jesus . . . proclaimed, 'If any one thirst, let him come to me and drink. He who believes in me, as the scripture has said, "Out of his heart shall flow rivers of living water."' Now this he said about the Spirit, which those who believed in him were to receive" (John 7:37-39).

"And I will pray the Father, and he will give you another Counselor, to be with you for ever, even the Spirit of truth, whom the world cannot receive, because it neither sees him nor knows him; you know him, for he dwells with you, and will be in you" (John 14:16-17).

"But when the Counselor comes, whom I shall send to you from the Father, even the Spirit of truth, who proceeds from the Father, he will bear witness to me" (John 15:26).

"I tell you the truth: it is to your advantage that I go away, for if I do not go away, the Counselor will not come to you; but if I go, I will send him to you" (John 16:7).

"I have yet many things to say to you, but you cannot bear them now. When the Spirit of truth comes, he will guide you into all the truth; for he will not speak on his own authority, but whatever he hears he will speak, and he will declare to you the things that are to come. He will glorify me, for he will take what is mine and declare it to you" (John 16:12-14).

"And behold, I send the promise of my Father upon you; but stay in the city, until you are clothed with power from on high" (Luke 24:49).

"And while staying with them he charged them not to depart from Jerusalem, but to wait for the promise of the Father, which, he said, 'you heard from me, for John baptized with water, but before many days you shall be baptized with the Holy Spirit' " (Acts 1:4-5).

"But you shall receive power when the Holy Spirit has come upon you; and you shall be my witnesses in Jerusalem and in all Judea and Samaria and to the end of the earth" (Acts 1:8).

"And Peter said to them, 'Repent, and be baptized every one of you in the name of Jesus Christ for the forgiveness of your sins; and you shall receive the gift of the Holy Spirit. For the promise is to you and to your children and to all that are far off, every one whom the Lord our God calls to him' " (Acts 2:38-39).

This promise of the Holy Spirit is therefore meant for every repentant, baptized child of God: for Jews and their descendants, and for the far-off Gentiles like you and me: it is for every one whom the Lord calls and saves!

7. *Don't proceed until you are hungry and thirsty for the Spirit's fullness on God's terms.* The Psalmist cried: "As the deer pants for the water brooks, so my soul pants for Thee, O God. My soul thirsts for God for the Living God" (Ps. 42:1-2, NASB; see 63:1-4). This should be our own prayer also, now and always.

One essential condition for being filled with the Holy Spirit is to have a deep hunger and thirst for God. Spiritual enrichment by its very nature cannot be imposed upon men, and for this reason when Jesus was speaking of the gift of the Holy Spirit He invited only the *thirsty* to come to Him and receive: "If anyone *thirst*, let him come to me and drink. He who believes in me, as the scripture has said, 'Out of his heart [inner being] shall flow rivers of living water' " (John 7:37-38).

Jesus makes the enjoyment of His blessings dependent not only upon coming to Him in faith, but upon thirst, or, as it is stated elsewhere, hunger and thirst: "Blessed are those who *hunger and thirst* for righteousness, for *they* shall be satisfied" (Matt. 5:6).

There is simply no substitute for this deep hunger and thirst for the Holy Spirit. It should be one of the deepest longings of your heart to be filled with Him. When a man is really thirsty for water he just can't be casual: he can't think about anything else. He can't settle for anything else. He becomes a desperate, determined man. He has one aim—to have his thirst quenched. He demands satisfaction. Others may waste water or underestimate its importance, but not the parched man, for he has grown to appreciate the precious value of its thirst-quenching qualities.

If you are content to remain without the gift of God you will not receive, but if you simply must have Him He will be found by you. Like Jacob the urgent cry of your heart must be, "I will not let you go unless you bless me!" (Gen. 32:26). Then, like Jacob, you too will be blessed; and blessed with a depth of experience that can only be from the Lord Jesus Christ.

You need to have a deep hunger and thirst, an urgency and longing, and a dissatisfaction with your present spiritual poverty without the fullness of God's Spirit. A man may be very aware of his need to be filled and yet still not have a deep yearning for the need to be met. He can be like an alcoholic who realizes his problem but is content to remain as he is. He may feel quite comfortable without further spiritual blessing, so God leaves him that way; for He does not cheapen His gifts by squandering them on those who feel no real need for them. He will not fill one who is not hungry, nor satisfy one who is not thirsty. He still fills *the hungry* with good things, but those who feel rich enough or content as they are, He sends empty away (Luke 1:53).

If you don't feel this need and desire, ask God to show you why. In the meantime don't ask for the gift of the Holy Spirit, for it is far better to delay asking until you can pray with conviction and with all your heart for His fullness. "You will seek Me and find Me when you search for Me with all your heart. And I will be found by you" (Jer. 29:13-14, NASB). Until you reach that point, your asking will be halfhearted and you will not be motivated to exercise sufficient faith to receive God's promise (see James 1:7-8). You will be easily put off. Moreover, until you manifest a real love and hunger for God's best gifts and take Him seriously, He cannot be expected to take you seriously.

On the other hand, you may be hungry and thirsty for God but so aware of your own unworthiness that you wonder whether God could bless you when you feel so dry, barren and inadequate in your Christian life. But remember that your very dryness and desire is a sign of His activity: "The grass withers, the flower fades, when the breath [Spirit] of the Lord blows upon it" (Isa. 40:7). The Spirit works in different but consistent ways. He first awakens us to an awareness of our dryness and need, and uncovers our inability to really worship God or minister to others at sufficient depth. In contrast He shows us His bountiful provision, and reveals all that He has made available for our refreshing and life. As we begin to perceive His goodness He moves upon us further to create the desire and thirst to actually partake of that which He is offering, so that we will not just look at the water available, but drink from its abundant supply.

In my own life there have been many passages that the Lord has graciously used to create a thirst for Him and for the fullness of the Spirit. There were the ones already listed in this chapter which showed me that the Spirit's fullness was for me personally. But there were many others, like the following:

"When the poor and needy seek water, and there is none, and their tongue is *parched* with thirst, I the Lord will answer them, I the God of Israel will not forsake them. I will open rivers *on the bare heights*, and fountains in the midst of the valleys; I will make *the wilderness* a pool of water, and *the dry land* springs of water . . . that men may see and know, may consider and understand together, that the hand of the Lord has done this" (Isa. 41:17-20).

"Behold, I am doing a new thing; now it springs forth, do you not perceive it? I will make a way *in the wilderness* and rivers *in the desert* . . . for I give water *in the wilderness*, rivers *in the desert*, to give drink to my chosen people, the people whom I formed for myself that they might declare my praise" (Isa. 43:19-21).

"For I will pour water *on the thirsty land*, and streams *on the dry ground*; I will pour my Spirit upon your descendants, and my blessing on your offspring" (Isa. 44:3).

In these verses God is not giving a horticultural lesson! He is describing how in any age He regards dry hearts that are like thirsty pastures ready to drink in His refreshing rain.

I well remember meditating upon these and similar scriptures after I had become convinced that, like many other Christians, I was not experiencing anything approaching the richness of life found in the New Testament. I really loved the Lord and was seeking to serve Him, but now He used these passages to show what was available in Him, and with this awareness I saw the contrast of my own spiritual dryness. I could well be described as a desert or a wilderness! But then the Lord showed me that if dryness was a qualification for receiving the outpouring of His Holy Spirit, I really qualified! God was not offering to pour out a deluge of the Spirit on the rich or the luscious green pastures that showed no signs of thirst, but upon the ones which had a great hunger and thirst for Him, and knew they needed a greater awareness of His presence, grace and power.

So if you feel dry and are yearning for the water of the Spirit, you also qualify! God has graciously placed His blessings on a shelf you can reach! You can proceed with great expectation!

18

Receiving the Promise

Receiving

Before we proceed may I suggest you forget all the dramatic stories you've heard of how others have received. Too often we hear only the sensational stories of conversion and baptism in the Spirit, and the impression may be given that the moment of reception will be marked by sensational or dramatic experiences. This is a mistake for the vast majority come to the Lord and are baptized in the Spirit in a way that is quiet but just as genuine. Those who have had dramatic experiences at the very moment of exercising faith could add that they then had to adjust to a basically unemotional level, which was sometimes hard for them to do, for it is easy to make the mistake of thinking something is wrong when the original feeling fades away. God had to bring them back to trusting solely in His Word, and building their lives upon it. The reality of your experience isn't determined by its dramatic content. Neither does your emotional experience need to duplicate another's to be genuine. It is wonderful if God gives you an emotional experience, but the Scriptures don't even mention this specifically in connection with baptism in the Spirit. The quiet act made in faith has very great potential. Remember that things are true and sacred not because they are dramatic or have emotional content, but because they come from God himself.

Perhaps you have a question as you anticipate receiving the Spirit. You may be puzzled when you recall the spontaneous way the disciples received the Spirit on the Day of Pentecost. They simply waited and were suddenly filled and spoke in tongues. There was no message, no instruction, no laying on of hands.

There are cases today where such a spontaneous initial filling occurs. But we should bear in mind that there is no record of fullness and tongues occurring again in exactly the same way as on the Day of Pentecost. Certainly there were four cases at least where God used men to preach, instruct and/or lay hands on those who received (Acts 8, 9, 10, 19). Also we need to remember that the preparation the 120 had received prior to being baptized in the Spirit was very different from that which we have. They had certainly not been indoctrinated to believe tongues were not for today, were suspect, and so on. They had all heard the wonderful teaching from none other than the Son of God himself, had seen His flawless life, His mighty miracles, and over very recent days had seen Him as the risen victorious Lord. Their hearts and spirits were wide open to anything their Master wanted to give and manifest through them. If we had received this same background experience, we probably would not need instruction either,

There is a battle on whenever you want to advance in the Christian life. Satan will oppose you, for he wants to keep you in unbelief and inactivity. If he can cause you discouragement, you will do nothing! He schemes to bring you back into complacency. So let nothing stand in your way! Be determined to receive from the Lord the blessing He offers you (see Luke 16:16). You can count on His definite help as you advance to receive the promise of the Father.

1. *Come to Jesus the Baptizer in the Holy Spirit.* Everything in the Christian faith centers around the Lord Jesus Christ. This is certainly the case concerning baptism in the Spirit, for Jesus himself is the Baptizer.

John the Baptist said, "I baptize you with water for repentance, but He who is coming after me is mightier than I, whose sandals I am not worthy to carry; *He* will baptize you with the Holy Spirit and with fire" (Matt. 3:11). John described Jesus as "the Lamb of God who takes away the sin of the world." He then repeated God's words concerning another important ministry of Jesus: "*This is he who baptizes with the Holy Spirit*" (John 1:29, 33). The same Savior who continues to take away sin also continues to baptize believers in the Spirit! These are both distinctive aspects of His ministry.

Peter said of Him: "This Jesus God raised up, and of that we are all witnesses. Being therefore exalted at the right hand of God, and having received from the Father the promise of the Holy Spirit, *he* has poured out this which you see and hear" (Acts 2:32-33). In speaking about receiving the Spirit, Jesus said: "If any one thirst, let him come to *me* and drink" (John 7:37).

To be baptized in the Spirit is not therefore to go *beyond* Christ but to be further occupied with Him who is the Baptizer.

In earlier generations, various other aspects of His person and work have been mentioned, but almost invariably His work as Baptizer has been glossed over, or regarded as the preserve of the theologian, and Jesus has been denied the glory which is His due. You, however, have the honor of seeking an encounter with Jesus the Lord and Baptizer, and of bringing glory to Him through what He will do in your life.

Jesus, then, is Lord, Savior, Faith-builder, Baptizer!

2. *Ask Jesus to baptize you in the Holy Spirit, receive the gift, and thank Him.* If it took you ten years of preparation to reach this point, it would be worth all those years! But you need not wait that long! You could well receive this very moment and before you have read another page! This is because sincerity, love, and a willingness to face the deep dealings of God provide the ideal environment for faith, hunger and thirst to mushroom under His touch. He is more eager than you are that you quickly receive the promise and speak to Him in tongues. His very nature longs to give and bless.

The Holy Spirit is received *by faith*, not by good works, struggling, pleading, or by enthusiasm and exuberance. "We . . . receive the promise of the Spirit *through faith*" (Gal. 3:14; see 3:2, 5). Jesus said: "He who *believes* in me, as the scripture has said, 'Out of his heart [inner being] shall flow rivers of living water.' Now this He said about the Spirit which those who *believed* in Him were to receive" (John 7:38-39).

The Holy Spirit is also received *by asking*, for Jesus said: "If you then, who are evil, know how to give good gifts to your children, how much more will the heavenly Father give the Holy Spirit [and good gifts] *to those who ask him?*" (Luke 11:13; Matt. 7:11).

After asking in faith you should stop asking and *receive* the Holy Spirit. The Spirit is not only asked for: He is received; that is, *taken* into your life (Acts 19:2; 8:15-17; 10:47). In illustration of this, Jesus likened the act of receiving the Holy Spirit to that of *drinking*, for He said: "If any one thirst, let him come to me and *drink*." This "drinking" represents a deliberate and active process of receiving, which you must do for yourself. No one can drink for you!

You will recall that when Jesus imparted the Spirit to His disciples, He *breathed* on them and said, "*Receive [take]* the Holy Spirit" (John 20:22). I can well believe that as Jesus breathed on them physically they found themselves breathing in (receiving, taking, drinking) as they responded and took the life of the Spirit into their innermost being. You may like to do the same.

It may seem unusual to you at the moment but it is very rewarding (and scriptural) to lift your hands in worship to the Lord. Just as kneeling expresses reverence and adoration, so arms raised with open and uplifted palms express openness, surrender, abandonment, devotion, humble dependence and obedience (1 Kings 8: 22; Neh. 8:6; Ps. 63:4; 134:2; 141:2; Lam. 3:41; 1 Tim. 2:8). It is the testimony of millions that this physical expression performed as a deliberate act of *will* has the power to activate faith and receptivity.

We are now ready to proceed with the prayer of invitation. You may like to pray in your own words, or you may prefer to pray this simple prayer:

"Heavenly Father, I thank you that the blood of Jesus, your Son, has cleansed me from every sin, and that Jesus himself has come into my life to be my Lord and Savior. I now open my life to you afresh, Lord Jesus, and ask you right now to baptize me in the Holy Spirit and let me praise you in a new language without the limitations of my intellect. I now receive your Holy Spirit, . . . and thank you for baptizing me in the Holy Spirit. Thank You, Lord Jesus. Amen."

I am absolutely convinced that when you pray a simple prayer like that and are open to the full ministry of Jesus Christ the Savior and Baptizer as revealed in Scripture, Jesus does in reality, right then and there, baptize you in the Holy Spirit. As a result you are filled with the Spirit and automatically given the supernatural ability to speak to the Lord in tongues, for the gift of tongues is given with baptism in the Spirit. You instantly acquire the ability to speak in tongues, and you can manifest it immediately. You have the gift, as it were, in cold storage! And, if you will, you can immediately take it out and exercise it.

It is not even essential to ask specifically for tongues, though there is nothing at all wrong with doing so! You need only pray to be baptized in the Spirit, and with this you will be given the ability to speak in tongues!

As you pray you may well become aware of the sweet nearness of the Lord, or of some other satisfying emotion. If so, rejoice and worship Him. On the other hand, you may be like the writer who asked in faith, thanked the Lord, and felt nothing!—other than a sense of rightness, and that this was in the perfect plan of God. I can't stress too much that we receive the Holy Spirit *by faith* and not by feeling (Gal. 3:14, 2, 5). Feelings will, however, certainly follow, but they may not come until days or weeks later when in your spirit you really do accept the reality of what has happened.

3. *Open your mouth and speak in faith.* The fullness is not an end in itself. Too often people have prayed to be filled with the Spirit and the matter has been left there.

Up in the hills beyond many cities there are huge reservoirs filled with fresh water which is able to meet a multitude of different needs and bring renewal and refreshing. But before the water can bring any benefits it has to be released. The giant faucets must be opened so that the huge pipes can be filled and the water conveyed to the needy city. The fullness of the reservoir with its vast potential and abundant supply of water may be all in order, but it is quite useless to the city until it is released and begins to flow. But when the water faucet is opened, the water gets away and brings refreshing and life to people and gardens and cleansing to the city. Until then fullness has no practical use.

Similarly, fullness of the Spirit is a "non-event"—a theological abstraction of academic interest only—until the mouth is opened and the pent-up praise and adoration is allowed to flow to the Lord. Only then do we become fully aware of the supply of the Spirit, the Living Water, and His mighty energizing effect.

Under the Christian dispensation fullness has as its initial outlet the gift of tongues. Therefore, when the Spirit comes within and fills the believer the faucet (tongues) needs to be turned on so that inspired praise from the Spirit can be released.

I'm personally convinced that Satan is undisturbed by people praying to be filled with the Spirit where it is divorced from expectancy and faith for the release of supernatural worship and enablement. Such limited understanding and appropriation provides little threat to him. It is the fullness of the Spirit with speaking in tongues which he detests and fights!

We earlier noticed how faith involves action in doing the revealed will of God. A helpful New Testament example of this is found in the story of Peter walking on the water to go to Jesus. Anyone who wants to be baptized in the Spirit can learn much from it, for the same faith principles apply.

When Jesus encouraged Peter to come to Him over the water, Peter had to take a series of completely human steps before this was possible. He first had to determine by an act of his will that he would leave the security of the boat and the environment that he knew so well, and trust himself to the Lord in a way he had never done before. He next had to make his body respond:

he had to stand up, move to the side of the boat, step out of it one leg after the other, and let go and trust God before He worked a miracle and enabled Peter to stay on top. The Lord would not impose a miracle upon him or move Peter's legs for him. He required Peter to do that himself by an act of his will, and without any assistance. But as soon as he had done what he could to co-operate with the revealed will of God, God took over and performed that which Peter could not do. The miracle began. Even then, however, Peter had to trust God and keep on walking for the miracle to continue: once he was on the water he didn't just stand with his feet together and get to Jesus by supernatural propulsion. He had to continue walking one leg after the other, and as he did so the miracle continued.

The Lord therefore did not work this miracle independently of man. Both were working together for it to take place.

The miracle of speaking in tongues is likewise not imposed upon you, and it too involves bringing your body into subjection and allowing yourself to speak, as you trust God for the release of your new language. This trust in God is one of the reasons why He makes the gift such a blessing.

In short, in answer to our prayer of faith Jesus baptizes us and provides us at that very moment with a new language. We can then immediately voice the new language we have been given, and our spirit can express itself as we magnify the Lord and rejoice in God our Savior. Yet God does not force us to speak immediately even though we could if we would! The miracle awaits the stepping out in faith, or the speaking in faith. Faith inherits the promises!

Remember that you cannot walk on water while you remain comfortably in the boat! And you cannot speak in tongues while you remain in the comfort and security of your English-language (or any other known language) boat! You have to get away from it before the miracle occurs. That may, of course, be an effort, but it will be abundantly worthwhile!

The Holy Spirit never speaks in tongues. He gives the release and the power of utterance but the responsibility to co-operate with Him rests with us: "*They* began to speak . . . as the Spirit gave *them* utterance" (Acts 2:4). "I want *you* all to speak in tongues." "*I* speak in tongues more than you all." "*I* will pray with the spirit and *I* will pray with the mind also" (1 Cor. 14:5, 18, 15). Praying with the spirit requires the same determined effort as does praying with the mind. It doesn't just happen! But when you *do* speak God inspires and guides the expression as He suggests the words to your mind.

It is impossible to speak in tongues unless you speak! So, as we have implied, to receive the ability to speak to the Lord in tongues it is essential that you are willing and determined to speak out in love and faith words that are not in any known language. Many people wait for the Spirit to take over and cause them to speak without any effort of their wills, but this does not occur. The Holy Spirit never over-rides a personality or forces any gift into operation. Rather, He waits until the believer is eager and determined to co-operate and is surrendered sufficiently to respond in faith in the direction of God's will. Then Jesus baptizes him in the Spirit, releases him to speak, and rewards his step of faith by giving the inspiration for the gift to flow.

So don't wait for a vision, a voice, some particular feeling, or for God to somehow bombard you with the words before you venture to speak in tongues. It seldom happens this way. You love the Lord. So tell Him so, in English and then in tongues. Trust Him and speak in faith the language He has given you. And don't be concerned about trying to speak quickly, for there is no special merit in that. The fluency of your utterance will look after itself as the language develops.

When you first gave your life to Christ and realized that He had died and risen to save you, the awareness of the essential part *you* had in repenting, believing and accepting Him by faith was in the forefront of your mind. But later you puzzled over His words: "You did not choose me, but I chose you" (John 15:16). You, like the disciples indeed chose the Lord, but suddenly the wonder of *His* earlier choice of you began to dawn on your spirit. Now you see that *before* you chose Him He had in grace taken the initiative, drawn you and made himself available so you could choose Him.

This is what happens when we speak in tongues. When we begin to speak it is all so new. We are often overwhelmingly conscious of our own endeavor, and it is just at this point that so many hesitate. They say to themselves: "This is just me. I'm doing this myself!", and with this thought they retreat and discard the very beginnings of their genuine new language. Yet if at this point they continued to speak, trusting God to increase their new language He would do so. In retrospect, if not at the time, they would be able to say with joy in the Lord and utter assurance: "I did not choose this language: it was chosen for me. I spoke in tongues as the Spirit gave me expression."

Perhaps like many others you can look back to the time when with sincerity and love but with a small faith you first invited the Lord Jesus Christ into your life. You may have thought: "This is just me saying this. I'm just imagining Jesus is there and will save me. I don't feel anything. I'm very conscious of the prayer I'm praying but not at all conscious that He is really answering. This is just wishful thinking." And maybe dozens of questions either then or later began to filter through your mind about the foolishness of what you were doing. But now your testimony as a Christian is that accepting Jesus Christ in cold faith and in accordance with the revealed will of God was far from foolishness. God really *did* answer! Jesus *was* there, and He *did* save and come into your life! His Word *could* be trusted! You may not have known assurance of salvation immediately, but if not, you knew later! The skeptic who ridicules the way of faith and rejects Christ understandably knows no such assurance, but you responded to God's revealed will and you *know* that Jesus saved you!

In the same way, although it is true that *you* are speaking in tongues (just as it was true that *Peter* was doing the walking), it is also true that because you have asked in sincerity and faith, the Holy Spirit has intervened in the situation, has transformed it, and is inspiring just those particular syllables you are expressing.

This, of course, is where the whole battle is fought—and no one can fight it for you. You have to decide whether you will or won't trust in God's faithfulness, knowing that He will give the Holy Spirit and good gifts to those who sincerely ask Him (Luke 11:11-13; Matt. 7:11). The Holy Spirit will prompt and inspire. Remember He wants you to pray in tongues more than you do, and He will move upon you to release this gift, whether you feel His touch or not (see John 20:29). *He* will choose your words and language, even though at the moment all you may be conscious of is your own effort. Later you will be able truthfully to say, "I did not choose those words; He chose them for me."

Above all, do not let distrust or anxiety rob you of His provision, nor permit unbelief to keep your mouth closed.

You may feel, however, that in spite of all that has been said you need outside help. If so, do not feel at all ashamed to request ministry from some trusted man or woman of God, not someone who wants to impose him or herself upon you, but one in whom you have confidence. Remember that even Paul who had met the risen Lord needed Ananias to pray for him with laying on of hands before he could receive the Holy Spirit (Acts 9:17-18;

see 8:15-18; 19:6). Through this ministry other needs may be met, any remaining barriers can be supernaturally revealed, faith and courage can grow, and you can be encouraged by the Lord to move forward and appropriate His gift.

Remember too, that whether you receive the Spirit and speak in tongues on your own or when prayed for by another, you are baptized in the Spirit not because your emotional level is heightened—there may in fact be no change—but because you have been brought into an entirely new and revolutionary dimension where inspired praise to the Lord is released from within your own spirit, and where the Holy Spirit has now increased opportunity to uncover and fill repeatedly.

You may not realize immediately the significance of all that has taken place, but you will soon find that, not only in theory but in reality also, a new dimension of the Spirit has been opened to you.

Continuing in Faith

It is not by accident we read how very soon after the Holy Spirit descended upon Jesus at His baptism, He was tempted by the devil (Luke 3:21-22; 4:1). If the Son of God was challenged in this way, then we can hardly expect to escape! Be prepared, for when you are baptized in the Spirit and speak in tongues Satan will be after you too. There is no need to be afraid of him because greater is He who is within you than he who is in the world (see 1 John 4:4), but be aware of his wiles. He will seek to take your legitimate enquiries, turn them into serious doubts, and then paralyze you so that you discontinue.

Once you have begun to speak in tongues *keep using your gift every day*, for it links you in spiritual worship with the Lord, creates a continuing attitude of openness to Him and strengthens you. There is little point in being able to pray in tongues if you don't continue to do so regularly, so plan on it becoming a daily lifelong habit, part of your life of faith (1 Cor. 14:15, 18; Eph. 6:18; Jude 20). Salvation operates by grace in response to our faith, not our feelings (Eph. 2:8-9), and the same is true of commencing and continuing to pray in tongues: it also is by grace through faith.

So when you feel like praying in tongues pray in tongues, for there is no better time to speak to God! And when you feel *least* like praying in tongues, when you feel terrible, under pressure, tempted, and without a sense of God's presence, pray in tongues then too for that is the perfect opportunity to be built up! Any time is the right time! For even in "unsuitable" situations you can pray effectively in tongues without a sound escaping your lips. Right from the beginning get into the habit of praying in the spirit as frequently as you can, for in doing this not only is the Lord glorified and you built up, but your gift is more firmly established while you do so (Col. 4:17; Jude 20). You will find that it will quickly become as natural as breathing to move from tongues to English and back to tongues as many times as you wish. *Above all, keep using it every day.*

If you are like most of us, you will soon find yourself asking, "Is my new language genuine? How can I be sure that these unusual words are really of God and pleasing to Him?"

Remember that He is absolutely trustworthy. You have committed yourself to the Lord, been guided by His Word, invited Him to baptize you in the Holy Spirit, and been open to Him. God is your Father, and has given His unchanging and sure word that He will give the Holy Spirit and good gifts to those who ask Him. His whole nature and name demand that He gives you nothing but the genuine.

Do not be discouraged or alarmed if your language is small at first. Some find a real release and flow in speech right from the beginning. But for others it is rather like a baby beginning to try his first words. At first the baby's words are halting and repetitive, and there is much deliberate effort in pronouncing them. But as he continues to speak, his vocabulary and fluency increase and he loses the sense of the mechanical effort of speech as it begins to flow naturally from him. Just as every syllable is music to the ears of his listening parents, so is every utterance in the spirit that ascends to our waiting heavenly Father.

From the start your utterance in tongues is likely to be completely of the Spirit. But if there are a few words which you recognize as imperfect, do not be concerned, for the Lord will quickly deal with them. Now that you have begun to move in the direction of the will of God, the Wind of the Spirit has freer access to the "sails of your yacht" and can blow upon them, change your direction more readily, and bring you fully into His course. If any words are imperfect or born of your human spirit, they will quickly drop away.

Some years ago a friend shared with us his sense of inadequacy regarding his early endeavors to pray in tongues. He told us that as he laid his few remaining doubts before the Lord he began to understand more clearly that his new language was really an offering. He then told the Lord: "Lord, it isn't much that I can give you with these halting words, but at the moment this is the very best gift I can bring. So I present it to you knowing you won't despise my offering, for it comes with all the love of my heart."

You can be sure with that spirit, it wasn't long before his language (which had been genuine right from the start) was really flowing freely, his witness for Christ was more positive and effective—indeed, it was transformed, and the love and joy of the Lord just radiated from him! God had certainly accepted his faith offering and was using him in a new way.

There are tremendous effects through the very "ordinary" and simple step of repenting and accepting Christ as Lord and Savior in faith. Similarly with this step of being baptized in the Spirit. But this is only the beginning of life in the Spirit and walking in the Spirit. There is much land to be possessed, much to be understood and appropriated, many battles to be fought and won. But He who has prepared and brought you to this new experience of Him will continue to go before and light the way. As you continue teachable, humble, and eager to love the Lord your God with heart, soul, mind and strength He will bring you fully into His purposes for your life.

Now after you have had time to consolidate your new language and are being built up by worshipping the Lord, share your testimony of what Jesus has done with other Christians who are open to God's moving. They will rejoice with you and together you can praise and thank the Lord in tongues and in English.

Also delve into the Word of God. God gave Spirit-baptized believers the books of Ephesians, Philippians, Romans—the whole New Testament, the whole Bible! Get into it and apply it! God has provided His truth for our spiritual health, learning and blessing. Every book of the Bible has its precious contribution which the Father wants to share with you. So be prepared continually to face the dealings of God as revealed there, for that is essential for your growth in maturity (see Job 22:21-30).

Jesus said: "You shall receive power when the Holy Spirit has come upon you; and you shall be my witnesses in Jerusalem and in all Judea and Samaria and to the end of the earth" (Acts 1:8). God blesses us that we might bless others. Today there are vast numbers who do not know the Lord Jesus Christ, and they need to know He died, rose again and is alive forevermore, and is still active in saving, helping, intervening and empowering in human situations. *He is Lord!* And it is our great privilege to share such life-transforming news!

And as we do so our trust is in the Lord. "And I am sure that he who began a good work in you will bring it to completion at the day of Jesus Christ" (Phil. 1:6).

A Personal Testimony

I am reluctant to refer to my own experience in a book like this, for it is very personal, and, in my view, no words can possibly express it. In addition, I want no one to consider this the pattern for them, for others' experiences may be very different yet still completely valid. However, if I say nothing further after stressing the importance of responding to the Lord in faith, there is the opposite danger of implying there was *only* a cold stepping out in faith, and nothing more. So I share briefly how the Lord was very gracious with me.

I loved the Lord and really wanted to serve Him more effectively. So when I became convinced it was His will for every Christian to be filled with the Spirit and speak in tongues, I began seeking Him for an increase in faith and for the same spiritual reality which the early Christians knew. And as I did so, a growing excitement began to fill my heart. This seeking continued for months, with an ever developing, yet strangely satisfying and exciting, hunger and thirst for God. When it came time for our summer vacation we went as a family to one of our beautiful New Zealand beaches, and during that time away from church responsibilities my search for the Lord continued. Over this period I would walk out on the beach by myself, surrender myself to God, and pray. It seemed as if I prayed earnestly in every posture known to man! Yet, for all my asking, nothing significant happened! At the end of that time of refreshing, family togetherness and seeking, I returned home hungrier than ever, convinced that God was teaching some important lessons through all this—but knowing I had still not received the reality I sought.

About two weeks later I had waited long enough! I just *had* to be filled with the Holy Spirit without any further delay! By now it had finally dawned on me that the Lord had been trying for some time to tell me it was my move next! I shut the study door, and, as I had done many times before, knelt down, asked to be filled, and thanked Him. But this time I started as deliberately as Peter had to get out of the treasured security of my English language boat. I saw no vision, heard no words, had no spontaneous flow of speech, felt no great rush of emotion. There was only the quiet exciting knowledge that by faith the Lord was with me at that very important moment in my life. In such an attitude of mind and heart I deliberately and in cold faith voiced to the Lord syllables and words that were unknown to me, and yet which gradually suggested themselves to my mind. As I did so I trusted the Lord to take them as a love offering and form them into a supernatural language of praise for His glory.

I had started in a calculated act of faith to express my love in words I could not understand, but because God and man are both involved in tongues I was at first unsure whether my new language was genuinely of the Spirit. It seemed too simple and too good to be true. At the same time it really *did* seem true! Yet during the following ten days of praying in tongues, my faith deepened until I finally knew with complete certainty, in my mind and deep in my spirit, that the tongue itself was indeed genuinely from God. I could see then that words which came to mind did so because the Holy Spirit himself had suggested them, prompted them.

Then all kinds of things began to happen! The Lord began to overwhelm me with a consciousness of His presence. Speaking in tongues became a glorious means of worship such as I had never known before. And all the while Jesus was there with me. I was standing on holy ground. The spiritual realm became suddenly more real. There was love such as I did not know I could contain. There was a deep flooding and overflowing with joy in God. There was a deep peace. I was bathed in, surrounded by, deluged with, washed through with the love of Jesus. I had previously known many times of wonderful communion with the Lord, but now He was revealing himself in a new and deeper way. As I said before, I knew that if this wasn't *the* baptism in the Holy Spirit, the Spirit of Jesus, it was certainly *a* baptism, an immersion in the love and grace and glory of God. For four days and nights this continued, and, especially at night when I could be still before the Lord, I could but worship Him in tongues, and sometimes in English, as I was swept by waves upon waves of the reality of the Lord. Near the end of this time I literally felt, and told the Lord, I could not take any more—but He allowed it to continue! Only gradually over a period of weeks did this subside.

Words cannot possibly convey the beauty and deliciousness of those days. At no time was there any change in my spiritual language, which convinces me that if I had only believed it was genuine right from the beginning, it would not have taken me ten days to reach the position where God could fully minister to my heart and spirit—but my faith had been small.

All this took place in early 1968. My only regret is that I resisted the Lord for so long and was limited in spiritual experience to the level my human mind could understand. I was an unbelieving believer. Since then there have been multplied occasions when the Lord has made himself real, but from that time of the Spirit's infilling a completely new dimension of supernatural worship and service began. It is no exaggeration to say my Christian experience and ministry to the Lord and others has to be divided into "before and after" the time I was first filled with the Spirit and spoke in tongues. From the first moment I determined to speak the syllables and words which suggested themselves to my mind, even in spite of some remaining doubts, a new dimension had been possessed in faith. I had earlier seen the promises from afar but now had walked out on this promised land and had claimed it. Or, to change the metaphor, with the Lord's help I had hoisted my sail and placed it in the path of the Wind of God. The new sense of closeness to Christ which followed soon after (when I really believed in my spirit His gift was genuine) was His further gracious confirmation of the spiritual reality which had occurred, but the initial step into this reality could be measured from the time ten days earlier when I had again committed myself to Christ, asked Him to fill or baptize me, and then expressed the words He quietly gave. That had been the crucial step of faith. The rest was the consequence.

This was the beginning of a new era in our Christian walk. (I can say "our," for three days later Joy also was filled with the Spirit, spoke in tongues and entered into the same new dimension.) Since then we have understood as never before what it means to be in the Body of Christ. Suddenly, also, we found there were riches in Christ and variety in serving Him which we had not known before. In all this, we felt, and still feel, we have only just begun. Often we have felt like excited and grateful spectators watching the Lord do many wonderful things, reclaiming lost lives, redirecting and empowering saved lives, and releasing prisoners' minds and personalities which Satan had bound. Only Christ himself can save and baptize people in the Holy Spirit and release their personalities to worship Him and pray in the Spirit, and then release other gifts within them. But we also know that this is exactly what He does.

To God alone be all glory and honor!

For teaching regarding spiritual gifts and the Bible's directives on their use, see the author's *Love and Gifts*.

Notes

Chapter 1

1. Acts 8:4-18. c. A.D. 32.
2. James D. G. Dunn, *Baptism in the Holy Spirit*, p. 71.
3. The metaphor of baptism is used to describe various experiences in the N.T., but whatever aspect is being considered, the common element is that all point to and involve a profound, life-altering and memorable reality.

Those who in earlier years had submitted to *Jewish proselyte baptism* testified in the act to a major change of religion and to a new allegiance, while *John's baptism* for the forgiveness of sins demanded profound and obvious change (Matt. 3:6-11a; Mark 1:4). Later, *Christian baptism* also expressed repentance, cleansing and death to self (Acts 2:38, 1 Pet. 3:21; 1 Cor. 6:11; Rom. 6:3-4). So too, *baptism into the Body of Christ* was one aspect of baptism that signified revolutionary obedience and separation from the ways of the unbelievers and adherance to a new company, the followers of Jesus. "Save yourselves from . . . " is followed by "They that received his word were baptized and . . . added" to the Church (1 Cor. 12:13; Acts 2:40-41).

Baptism in fire points to the powerful, consuming, purifying work of God when He burns away the chaff (Matt. 3:11-12; Heb. 12:29). *The baptism of power* (Acts 1:5, 8) and *of suffering* (Mark 10:38-39; Luke 12:50; John 18:11), of *baptism into [eis] the name* (ownership and possession) *of Jesus Christ* (Acts 8:16; 19:5; 1 Cor. 1:13) and *into the death and resurrection of Christ* (Rom. 6:1-4) similarly emphasize the depth and often the cataclysmic effect of the encounter. There was nothing vague, nebulous or merely theoretical about these baptisms.

Thus we may deduce from N.T. usage of the word baptism, as well as the actual examples of "baptism in the Spirit" that this latter term is also used to express the very deep and profound encounter with the living Spirit.

4. L. D. Guy, *Towards a New Testament Understanding of Baptism in the Spirit*, p. 2f.
5. Man has rebelled and his direction is downhill and away from God.

He is on the road to destruction. It is unnecessary for him actively to *take* condemnation for he is condemned already. He need do nothing but drift, for *he is automatically wide open to receive* the harvest of that way of living. *He refuses to come to Christ for life* (John 5:40). On the other hand, though dependent on grace, *blessings must be positively received.* If he would *take* or *receive* Christ, life, the Holy Spirit and the multiplicity of His additional favors, there must be deliberate endeavor—repentance, a change of direction, eager appropriation. He must either actively *take* or his whole attitude must be one of active co-operating openness to *receive* God's proferred enrichments. Wherever *lambanō* is used for receiving *any* precious gift of God, we notice how man's ardent response or total openness is involved, for God never cheapens His grace by imposing it upon reluctant, passive or faithless recipients.

The usual rendering of Acts 2:38: "Repent, and be baptized . . . and *you shall receive* the gift of the Holy Spirit" is an accurate and preferred translation of the future indicative of *lambanō*. Removed from its context it is just possible to translate as "Repent, and be baptized . . . and *take/ receive* [*you*] . . . the gift of the Holy Spirit," for the future indicative sometimes carries the force of an imperative, as in Luke 1:13: "*Thou shalt call* [*call thou*] his name John." (See also Matt. 1:21; 5:48; 6:5; 19:18-19; 22:37, 39; 1 Cor. 9:9, etc.) In its context, however, such a translation must be ruled out, for the future indicative follows two imperatives, and we could expect that Luke would have used a further imperative if he wanted us to understand it as such.

It is, however, quite unnecessary to change the usual " . . . you shall receive . . . ," for Peter's words were given to a specific people who were prepared, convicted, eager, co-operative and totally open to receive the Spirit whom they had seen and heard. The promise of the Spirit would be open to Peter's listeners, their children, and Gentiles—to all whom the Lord called. Yet the actual time of receiving the promise would vary. Some would in fact receive *before* their baptism, others after a delay and human intervention. But because Peter's present audience was so open hungry and thirsty to take the Spirit within them with His accompanying supernatural manifestations, He would be given and received immediately. To that particular congregation he could therefore say in effect: "Repent, and be baptized . . . and there is nothing surer than that you shall receive the gift of the Holy Spirit." It was God's will that they receive the Spirit, and in the unlikely event that any of them did not in fact receive Him immediately, the church leaders could no doubt have been guided to pray for them as they were later to do with the Samaritans and Ephesians.

6. For general discussion of the Samaritan episode, see *Love and Gifts*, pp. 103-106.

James Dunn makes the surprising assertion that what Simon and the Samaritans believed from Philip's message was not that Jesus was Lord and Savior but that He was the Samaritan Messiah who was about to usher in their long-awaited second kingdom. He feels that Philip could unconsciously have misled them into thinking that Jesus was about to set up an earthly kingdom which would unite all Israel, crush her enemies and exalt the Samaritan people—and that the Spirit was delayed because their "belief" (Acts 8:12-13) was of this barren inadequate variety (op. cit., 63f.).

This explanation is unconvincing. Philip was a responsible man, esteemed by the apostles and the Church, filled with the Spirit and wisdom (Acts 6:3). He was faithfully preaching the Word of God, the kingdom of God, and Jesus Christ (vv. 14, 12)—no doubt the same message (kērygma) that the apostles preached, declaring Jesus as Lord, Savior and God's Anointed, who had come to set up God's *spiritual* kingdom in the hearts of all who would respond to His lordship (Rom. 10:9-10). Then the Samaritans responded to his message, and he was willing to baptize them. As a Spirit-filled evangelist he would not give the Samaritans a completely false hope in an earthly kingdom, for that would pander to their pride and diametrically oppose the whole basis of salvation in Christ. Also, when Peter and John came, there is no suggestion that they were unhappy with Philip's message, or with the Samaritans' repentance, understanding of the gospel, trust in Christ, or Christian baptism. Neither was there any need for them to reteach or rebaptize. The Samaritans sole need was for the Spirit who had not yet fallen on them. All other aspects were satisfactory—with the one exception of Simon, where the problem was exposed and dealt with. Had there been any other basic problems they too would have been exposed.

The Samaritans' belief was clearly true Christian belief.

7. When at a later date Paul wrote to the Ephesians, he was well aware that their sealing with the Spirit (that is, their receiving of the Spirit) had been neither simultaneous with the commencement of true Christian faith nor with their ensuing baptism, but followed very soon afterwards when Paul laid hands upon them. A valid and preferred translation of Eph. 1:13 is therefore: "In him you also . . . after you believed in him were sealed with the promised Holy Spirit." All grammarians agree that the antecedent action of the aorist participle is more common, and the delay between Acts 19:5 and 6 (to say nothing of the earlier delay) would make that the preferred rendering here. Yet sometimes the aorist participle refers to coincident action (see *Love and Gifts*, p. 171f.), in which case we could translate: "On believing in Him [belief being understood as comprising repentance, belief, baptism, receiving the Spirit] you were *sealed* with the promised Holy Spirit." In this case "believing" is the response word which gathers together and represents all the various aspects of initiation (e.g., Acts 4:4; 5:14; 9:42; 13:12).

Paul would have to say as a simple statement of fact, that he, the twelve Ephesians, the Samaritans, and even the original 120 were sealed *after* they first believed and became regenerate and forgiven. On the other hand, as noted above, even though in experience the various ingredients of initiation were briefly separated, they could also be viewed as a unified whole, in which case it could also be said: "On believing in him you were sealed." Yet while there was more commonly a delay, Paul would with the Cornelius' event in mind, no doubt believe that sealing could sometimes happen simultaneously with conversion, or be so closely linked with the commencement of saving faith that it was neither needful nor practical to differentiate between the events (see Acts 10:44-48). Paul's reference in Eph. 1:13 is wide enough to comprise both those who received the Spirit after saving belief, or simultaneously with it.

8. Cf. ARV & NIV translations. The Western text reads, "We have never even heard whether people are receiving the Holy Spirit." In a similar way it amplified John 7:39, to read, "for the Spirit was not yet *given.*" F. F. Bruce comments: "Even if they had only been baptized with John's baptism, they conceivably knew that John had spoken of a coming baptism with the Holy Spirit; they did not know, however, that this expected baptism was now an accomplished fact" (see *Book of the Acts*, p. 385f.).

9. It is sometimes forgotten that when Paul said that he and his Christian readers were "complete in Christ" and "blessed in Christ with every spiritual blessing" (Col. 2:10, KJV; Eph. 1:3), he was not referring to the unbaptized or those who had not personally been flooded with the Spirit. Any idea that we are complete in Christ regardless of obeying Him in baptism fails to do justice to the important place this sacrament has within the N.T. Baptism is not a meaningless, valueless or merely picturesque adjunct to personal commitment. It is an important occasion where the grace of God touches and ministers further to those who have determined to follow Him. To apply the idea of completeness to those only partially initiated creates confusion, which can in turn quickly settle into complacency.

Yet initiation is only the beginning, for by the wonder of God's grace there is always the forward aspect of hungering and appropriating, of subsequent and repeated infillings and supplies of grace, that the Father's blood-bought children might increasingly reveal, enjoy and serve Him. How ever much grace we have received, "He gives more . . . "! (James 4:6; see 2 Pet. 1:2).

10. Although there are many places where baptism is not mentioned at all, F. F. Bruce is fully justified in saying, "The idea of an unbaptized Christian is simply not entertained in N.T." (*Book of the Acts*, p. 77).

11. Baptism and reception of the Spirit are unrecorded in places in Acts where we could fully expect them to be mentioned had Luke described in detail what happened when people believed.

Baptism is unrecorded in Acts 2:1-4, 47; 4:4; 5:14; 6:7; 9:31, 32-35, 42; 11:20-21, 22-24; 12:24; 13:12, 48-49; 14:1, 21; 16:5; 17:1-4, 10-12, 32-34; 19:17-20.

Reception of the Spirit is unrecorded in Acts 2:41-42, 47; 4:4; 5:14; 6:7; 8:34-39; 9:31, 32-35, 42; 11:20-21, 22-24; 12:24; 13:12, 48-49; 14:1, 21; 16:5, 14-15, 30-34; 17:1-4, 10-12, 32-34; 18:8; 19:17-20.

12. It is without foundation to argue that the Spirit of Christ (*pneuma Christou*) refers in Rom. 8:9; to "a Christian or a Christlike spirit." The Spirit of Christ is none other than the Holy Spirit who witnesses to Christ. He is the Spirit of the Lord, of Jesus Christ, and of God (Acts 8:39; 16:7; Phil. 1:19).

13. C. H. Dodd, *Epistle of Paul to the Romans* (italics mine). See also J. D. G. Dunn, op. cit., pp. 66, 71, 105, 113, 121, 132f., 138, 149, 172, 225f.

14. "The receiving of the Holy Spirit in Acts is connected with the manifestation of some spiritual gift" (F. F. Bruce, *Acts of the Apostles*, p. 187). In commenting on Rom. 8:9, Leslie Allan writes: "The decisive test of belonging to Christ is possession of the Spirit which is demonstrable (cf. Acts 10:45f.), being outwardly verified by evidence of His gifts (cf. 1 C. 12:4-11) and/or of His fruit" (*A New Testament Commentary*, p. 356). While equally convinced that fruit was essential and was an evidence of the Spirit's working, it was clearly not, however, the immediate evidence of receiving the Spirit in the early Church. See Ch. 9 of this book, and the author's *Love and Gifts*, p. 173 (note 7).

15. J. D. G. Dunn, op. cit., pp. 133, 172.

16. By the time Paul met Ananias he had been convicted of sin (Acts 9:5; 26:14), had believed in the resurrection of Christ and had seen the risen Lord (Rom. 10:9; Acts 22:14), had called Jesus "Lord" in the true sense (Acts 22:10; see 1 Cor. 12:3), was responsive to Him and prayerful (Acts 9:6, 8, 10; 22:10-11), and was commissioned by Christ (Acts 26:16-18). Also, when Ananias came he did not preach the gospel to Paul or pray that he might be saved, presumably because it was unnecessary (Acts 9:17; 22:14-16). Ananias called Paul "brother" and prayed for him that he might be filled with the Spirit (Acts 9:17; 22:13); and as the unregenerate cannot receive Him (John 14:17), this too confirms that he was already a regenerate believer.

17. Thomas A. Smail, *Reflected Glory*, p. 33.

18. Ibid. 148f. Smail quotes Simon Tugwell: "While we may agree . . . that Christianity plus is no longer Christianity, Pentecostalism has come in protest against Christianity minus" (*Did You Receive the Spirit?*, [Paulist-Newman] 1973, p. 87f.).

19. Heb. 6:1-2 mentions the basic steps which all new believers were expected to take, and the foundational truths they must believe. "Baptisms" covers both baptism in water and in the Spirit, the association of thought with the laying on of hands making this meaning clear. "Ablutions" and "washings" in some translations are inadequate renderings of *baptismōn* ("of baptisms"). *Baptismos* is not the usual word for Christian baptism but it is so used in some weighty texts in Col. 2:12. Reference to both baptisms is included in the plural form here.

Chapter 2

1. Within Scripture there is a very close connection between belief, baptism and baptism in the Spirit. Yet it is impossible in the light of the biblical records to say with F. D. Bruner that "Repentance is being baptized," "Baptism is Pentecost," and "Baptism becomes the baptism of the Holy Spirit" (A Theology of the Holy Spirit, pp. 166, 168. See also pp. 169-170).

2. Cf. From Jordan to Pentecost by Derek Prince, undated (Derek Prince Publications), p. 74.

3. George Beasley-Murray suggests that the Samaritan Christians in Acts 8 were not without the Spirit but without the spiritual gifts that characterized the common life of the Christian communities (see Baptism in the New Testament, 1962, Macmillan, p. 119). This view rightly acknowledges the prevalence of gifts but it is still inadequate. A careful writer like Luke would never expect his readers to understand the words "had not received the Spirit" to mean "had received the Spirit, but were without the characteristic manifestations." For him, as for all Christians, no appropriate manifestation meant the Spirit himself had not been received. Conversely, once the manifestation was present, Luke could state categorically that the Spirit had in fact been received. Early baptized believers were regenerate by the Spirit's power, yet without His indwelling, until such time as the release of appropriate spiritual gifts indicated that He had taken up residence.

Chapter 3

1. See pp. 66-67.

2. There are five further references to fullness of the Spirit. In these the fullness is linked with wisdom, faith and joy and possibly grace and power, wonders and signs (Acts 6:3, 5, [v. 8?]; 11:24; 13:52). Luke knew his Christian readers would understand that fullness of the Breath of God in these cases was associated with a supernatural increase in wisdom and faith and with joy at seeing God breaking into a situation in an obvious way. For our present purpose of understanding fullness and its effects, however, it is best to look to the primary passages mentioned earlier in the main text, for in the above references Luke is content to state only that fullness and wisdom, faith and joy were present together in the same people.

Chapter 5

1. Jesus had already at this time risen in power and returned to the Father, though not for the final time. The Ascension was His final departure to the Father, the conclusion of His visible dealings with men. (See F. F. Bruce, Book of the Acts, p. 40.) There was therefore no reason why the disciples could not receive the Holy Spirit then as well as in fullness at Pentecost.

Chapter 6

1. "Demons" is the correct translation of the word *daimones* which Irenaeus used.

2. *Against Heresies*, II. 32. 4; V. 6. 1 (italics mine). Eusebius in his *Church History* (V. Chapter 7) later quotes these passages from Irenaeus.

3. *Against Marcion*, V. 8 (italics mine). Quotations from Irenaeus and Tertullian are reprinted from *Ante-Nicene Fathers*, I. 409, 531; III. 446-447.

4. D. Bridge and D. Phypers, *Spiritual Gifts and the Church*, p. 29.

5. Ibid., 28.

Chapter 7

1. C. K. Barrett observes that when Paul expresses a wish he knows to be unattainable, he (rightly) uses the imperfect tense of *thelō* or *euchomai* (e.g., Gal. 4:20; Rom. 9:3). Conversely, when he uses the present tense to convey his desire for others (as in 1 Cor. 14:5 and numerous other places), he is expressing a wish that is capable of realization and ought to be realized. It has almost the force of a command. (See *First Epistle to the Corinthians*, p. 158). Thus in 1 Cor. 14:5 Paul was using his apostolic authority to say to his readers: "I want you all to speak in tongues. I know you can, and I expect you to do so."

2. Why does Paul say "I want you all to speak in tongues" when he knew that all Spirit-baptized believers could already do so? There are two alternatives: (i) Paul now says to Christians who could already speak in tongues in their own worship: "I want you to be open to the Lord's anointing so that from time to time you can all speak in tongues in authoritative public utterance which can then be interpreted, and which will bring the same edification as prophecy." I personally do not consider this is the point Paul is making here, even though all must be always ready to be used publicly in this way if God anoints them to do so. (ii) The present infinitive ("to speak in tongues" in this verse) "is only employed when attention is to be drawn to the prolonging or repetition of the action" (Eric Jay, *New Testament Greek*, p. 101). Paul is saying: "Let nothing turn you aside from God's provision. I want you all to use regularly God's gifts to you. I want you all to keep up the practice of speaking in tongues." It is not enough to have the ability to assemble together as God's people, pray with the mind and the spirit, and partake of the Supper if, in fact, this is no longer done. Paul is stressing continuity to people who already had this gift, some of whom may have been tempted to pray less and less in tongues or to leave speaking in tongues and go on to the more dramatic gifts.

Obviously, if they were all to continue to speak in tongues it was clearly God's will for them to have originally received the gift. The continuing assumes an initial reception. Similarly, "Be filled with the Spirit" and "Pray at all times in the Spirit" (Eph. 5:18; 6:18) have a continuous sense. There is no implication that these were impossible earlier. They too are calls to continuance.

3. E. K. Simpson and F. F. Bruce, *Epistles to the Ephesians and the Colossians*, p. 219f.

4. For scripture references, see these "Notes" on Chapter 1, note 11.

5. 1 Cor. had been written well before Luke wrote Acts. Therefore, aside from all other sources of information, Paul's and the Corinthians' speaking in tongues was widely known.

Chapter 8

1. See the author's *Love and Gifts*, pp. 149, 173.

2. In the context of Acts 10:27 *pollous* can be translated "many persons, large gathering." With 120 on the Day of Pentecost, plus the 12 Ephesians, even if there were only 28 people who received this sign at Caesarea, that would make a total of 160. However, use of the word *pollous* on that occasion could indicate a much larger gathering, in which case the hypothetical 28 is very conservative. A considerably higher figure cannot be ruled out, considering Cornelius' position, the respect with which he was obviously held, his sincerity, largeheartedness and obvious desire to share any word from the Lord. Yet whatever the number, they all spoke in tongues.

3. See the author's *Love and Gifts*, p. 105. Even if *logos* is here translated "matter" it can retain the meaning, "You have neither part nor lot in this matter which is being expressed."

4. Harold Horton, *The Baptism in the Holy Spirit*, p. 19f. (italics mine).

5. It could be added that if some who have had an initial experience of speaking in tongues do not go on to glorify Christ in other ways, that is no proof that the gift of tongues is unnecessary, a distraction, substitute, or whatever. It simply means that those people have for some reason failed to fulfill their responsibility to respond to the Lord in some areas of their lives. Exactly the same thing could be said concerning people who genuinely trust in Jesus Christ and are, therefore, born again, but fail to grow in grace as they could and should, and who often are, in consequence, pointed out by unbelievers as reasons for the Christian faith being unattractive or a hypocritical system. It would be foolish indeed to suggest that their lack proved that conversion did not glorify Christ, and could therefore be dispensed with. It would be equally illogical to argue that a failure to go on in the new experience of the Holy Spirit proved that such an experience was thereby proved useless or invalid.

6. For full quotation see Chapter 6. All Christians are in one sense complete or mature because of their incorporation into Christ and the Spirit (Col. 1:28), and it is this to which Paul refers in 1 Cor. 2:6-12. They are complete in that while there is much need for building and growth (1 Cor. 3:1) yet the great Christian foundation (of belief in Christ, baptism and receiving the Spirit) has been fully laid.

Chapter 9

1. Under the New Covenant, regular prophecy (which brings edification, encouragement and consolation) was destined to make an important contribution to spiritual life. Yet prophecy in its wider application could denote all divinely inspired revelation and speech. (See *Love and Gifts*, p. 26.) Peter therefore readily understood speaking in tongues as fulfilling Joel's words, "I will pour out my Spirit upon all flesh, and your sons and daughters shall *prophesy*" (Acts 2:15-17). The outpouring was thus marked by prophetic, God-given speech, but of an unusual kind, namely, inspired speech in tongues. (See F. F. Bruce, *Book of the Acts*, p. 56.) Regular prophecy could of course follow later but this was seen as the initial fulfillment.

2. Some may wonder how the Church could ever regard tongues as the initial sign of Holy Spirit baptism when in one rather condensed passage they are said to be "a sign not for believers but for unbelievers" (see 1 Cor. 14:21-22). It should be sufficient to make the following points:

(1) These words must be interpreted within their context. Paul was saying that tongues are a sign of separation and of judgment not for believers who respond to God but to unbelievers who rebel and will not listen to Him. (See *Love and Gifts*, p. 79f.) The Apostle was recalling the particular time in Israel's history when in punishment for her unbelief and rebellion God allowed the Israelites to be overrun by the Assyrian invaders whose strange tongues were then heard everywhere. Ancient and unbelieving Israel had had the bitter and humiliating experience of having to put up with seeing God give victory and joy to others, and with seeing and hearing the invaders possessing the land that they themselves should have been enjoying. Paul was compressing much into a small space but his overall thought is clear: to the unbelieving who resist God's will the presence of tongues in their midst ought to be seen as it really is, a token of God's gracious intervention, given to lead them to repentance. But just as Israel continued in her rebellion, so unbelievers today can choose to do the same. In such a condition the sound of tongues in their midst remains as an obvious sign or indication that even while God is blessing others, they, as unbelievers, stand outside His blessing and under His judgment. For believers, however, tongues do not represent such a sign; that is, they are not a sign of God's judgment upon them. We cannot therefore apply this verse to the quite unrelated question of whether tongues were the initial or even a subsequent sign of receiving the Holy Spirit.

(2) Although the word "sign" is absent, the thought of tongues as a sign *amongst believers* is conspicuous in various places. Tongues, for example, provided believers with a clear sign that God was at work among them (e.g., 1 Cor. 12:8-10); they were a sign that believers were speaking to the Lord in prayer under the Spirit's inspiration (e.g., 1 Cor. 14:2); and they obviously signified that the believers were not so perfect as to be beyond the need for upbuilding! (1 Cor. 14:4). Beyond

this, believing onlookers as well as believing participants knew because of the sign of speaking in tongues that the Holy Spirit had been poured out and was now present with them (Acts 10:45-47; 19:6; also 2:12-17, 33). The plain unambiguous testimony of these various scripture passages leaves us in no doubt that the early Church regarded tongues as a sign of God's activity among believers, and, when first given to a believer, as a convincing sign of Holy Spirit baptism.

3. Thomas A. Smail, op. cit., p. 134.

4. See A. Bittlinger, *Gifts and Graces*, p. 49f.

5. See *Love and Gifts*, pp. 72-75.

6. See, for example, *Thy God Reigneth*, by R. Edward Miller, 1964 (World M.A.P., 900 Glenoaks, Burbank, CA. 91502).

7. Even in more recent times B. B. Warfield seriously misunderstood N.T. teaching on gifts and ministries and their purpose, and argued in his well-known polemic, *Counterfeit Miracles*, that all modern claims to speaking in tongues must of necessity be spurious and dangerous! They are found only in the lunatic fringe of Christendom! Such expressions as these and the attitudes that prompted them show that anyone who mentioned that they spoke in tongues faced the real probability that their testimony would be rejected and their ministry brought to an end.

8. See ch. 7.

9. See ch. 3.

Chapter 11

1. A. W. Tozer, *That Incredible Christian*, p. 78.

Chapter 13

1. The Greek words rendered "interpretation" (*hermēneia* and *diermēneia*) refer to the explanation, interpretation or translation of spoken or written words (Luke 24:27; Acts 9:36; John 1:42; 9:7; Heb. 7:2). When mentioned in connection with tongues, however, "interpretation" or "the explanation of the meaning of tongues" are more suitable renderings of the Greek, for they suggest an endeavor to communicate the spirit and content of the original rather than offering an exact word for word translation. Yet whatever word is preferred it should be remembered that the interpreter no more understands the tongue than does the speaker.

2. See *Love and Gifts*, p. 62f.

3. Many pentecostals agree that tongues and interpretation are always prayer. See, for example, *The Spirit Bade Me Go*, by David J. du Plessis (Oakland: David J. du Plessis, n.d.), pp. 82-85.

Chapter 14

1. M. R. Vincent, *Word Studies in the New Testament*, pp. 791, 168.

2. C. K. Barrett, op. cit. 329, and *Epistle to the Romans*, p. 238.

3. F. F. Bruce, *Book of the Acts*, p. 242.

4. From *Bodmer Papyri* 13, para. 100ff.

Chapter 16

1. John R. W. Stott, *Baptism and Fullness*, pp. 15, 30. In this recent revision of an earlier book, Mr. Stott explains his position: "What is descriptive is valuable only insofar as it is interpreted by what is didactic. Some of the biblical narratives which describe events are self-interpreting because they include an explanatory comment, whereas others cannot be interpreted in isolation but only in the light of doctrinal or ethical teaching which is given elsewhere" (ibid. 15).

Although it may be arguable as to the extent of any special features in, say, the Samaritan and Ephesian accounts, they still retain value for what they reveal of the *regular* pattern found among other Christians, and for showing us the end result of the apostles' ministry on these occasions. The words and actions of others, plus Luke's own choice of words as to the state of the people being discussed, illustrates what constituted the normal and how the present cases were normalized. These events in Acts are self-interpreting because they do in fact include Luke's explanatory comments. Furthermore, the doctrine these passages teach is consistent with teaching given elsewhere, and is explained in the main text of this chapter, and especially in point 7.

2. It is surprising to find that those who claim doctrine should not be derived from narrative or descriptive passages, themselves build doctrine on their own selection of Acts passages which occur in the midst of narrative sections (e.g., Acts 2:38-39), and which they interpret to bear up their own doctrine (e.g., ibid. 22, 25-31)! Yet even if we overlook this practice, to teach from Acts 2:38-39 that forgiveness and the Holy Spirit *were and still are necessarily and always received at the same moment* is to go well beyond what that passage says or requires. It ignores the fact that there were major differences of background, conviction, and preparation, between Peter's original audience and people today, and, in any case, it is a doctrinal interpretation contradicted by scripture itself. It is valid to argue that though there may be brief gaps between them, belief, baptism and reception of the Spirit should be regarded as different parts of a single initiation into Christ: it is another thing entirely, and contrary to scripture, to argue that they *cannot* be separated (ibid. 36). They clearly *were* separable.

3. E.g., ibid., 30f.

4. James Denney, *Jesus and the Gospel*, p. 26f.

Chapter 17

1. Throughout his book, F. D. Bruner has confused qualifications with works (op. cit., 161f, 183f, etc.). In this he is completely out of touch with the New Testament. The Lord does not confer peace, forgiveness, freedom, life, or the Holy Spirit irrespective of the recipient's attitude. Jesus saw repentance, baptism, obedience, faith, hunger and thirst not as works of the flesh, heresy, or opposition to the way of grace. They were necessary conditions which He himself imposed. They were faith in action! Bruner's

constant portrayal of pentecostalism as a law system that contrasts with the gospel is incredible and indicates a complete lack of understanding of the basic pentecostal position, which does not and is never meant to suggest that the sinner in any way whatever earns the saving grace and power of God. One is left wondering whether Bruner would dare contemplate preparing his own soul as he seeks communion with God in prayer and worship lest he commit the fundamental error of hoping to earn God's grace by his own works! It is a fallacy to argue that grace is somehow diminished if we are responsive and eager to receive it! (See. Matt. 5:6; 15:22-28; Luke 1:53.)

Bruner is also critical of John Wesley, C. Finney, R. A. Torrey, Andrew Murray, A. J. Gordon and F. B. Meyer's doctrine of the Spirit and the preparation they suggest for a deeper experience in God. His position reveals a basic misunderstanding of New Testament teaching on how the grace of God is made effective.

Any reader questioning the validity of preparing for a deeper experience of God, or confused by the biblical relationship between faith and works, is directed to the very practical booklet, *Paths to Power* by A. W. Tozer (Christian Publications, Inc.).

2. A highly recommended book for those who have been involved in any occult area is *Angels of Light?* by Hobart E. Freeman (Logos International, 1969).

Index of Selected Scripture References

Page references for the companion volumes *Love and Gifts* and *Experiencing the Holy Spirit* are printed in regular and italic type respectively.

OLD TESTAMENT

162

NEW TESTAMENT

164

166